INDIA CHANGES!

INDIA CHANGES!

Taya Zinkin

*'I want cultures of all lands
to be blown about my house as freely as possible.
But I refuse to be blown off my feet by any.'*
—MOHANDAS K. GANDHI

1958
CHATTO AND WINDUS
LONDON

Published by
Chatto and Windus Ltd.
42 William IV Street
London, W.C.2

© *Taya Zinkin 1958*

Originally published by Oxford University Press, Inc., New York

TO MY PARENTS

ACKNOWLEDGEMENTS

I am grateful to Messrs. D. MacLachlan, G. Wint, A. Hetherington, and A. P. Wadsworth without whose encouragement over years I would never have written at all.

The ideas which have gone into the book have come from innumerable people. I owe a quite special debt to Mr. B. Venkatappiah; to Mr. H. M. Patel, to his wife and all their daughters. I would also like to mention the late Mrs. J. Taylor, Mrs. Scarlett Trent, Mrs. Dandekar, Dr. Stella Kramrisch, Mrs. Pupul Jayakar, Mrs. Indira Gandhi, Mrs. Mira Chaudhuri, Lady Krishnamachari, The Rani Saheba of Akalkot, Mrs. S. D. Deshmukh, Mrs. Ratna Ambegaonkar, Lady Rama Rao, Miss Sita Chari, Mrs. Fori Nehru, Mrs. J. F. Sinclair, Lady Srivastava, Mrs. Azim Hussein, Dr. A. K. Vasumati, Mrs. Tarkeshwari Sinha, Miss P. J. Havaldar, Mrs. L. R. Kumar, Mrs. Susheela Iengar, Mr. and Mrs. P. L. Tandon, Mr. and Mrs. S. Natarajan, Mr. and Mrs. E. Wood, Dr. Rajendra Prasad, Messrs. C. Rajagopalachari, Morarji R. Desai, U. N. Dhebar, Sir V. T. Krishnamachari, Mr. T. T. Krishnamachari, Pandit H. N. Kunzru, Sardar K. M. Panikkar, Messrs. C. S. Venkatachar, V. K. Ramaswami, D. S. Bakhle, M. V. Rangachari, Maharaj Nagendra Singh, Messrs. M. J. Desai, H. V. R. Iengar, A. D. Gorwala, Manzoor Qadir, Dr. B. K. Madan, Messrs. Hari Singh, J. B. Bowman, B. P. Dalal, B. B. Mundkur, Vijay Merchant, K. H. Vaswani, A. S. Menon, Prof. D. R. Gadgil, Prof. McKim Marriot, Mr. Hari Makkhan, and others.

In addition, Prof. M. N. Srinivas, Messrs. S. D. Deshmukh, B. Venkatappiah, H. M. Patel, Lovraj Kumar, M. K. Gangadharan, and Mrs. M. Toohey were kind enough to read through and comment upon my manuscript at various stages. Had it not been for their ready sacrifice of their time and effort, this book would have contained many more errors than it does. For any errors it may still contain I, and not they, am of course solely responsible.

I am grateful to the late Mr. A. P. Wadsworth and to Mr. A. Hetherington for permission to use material which first appeared as articles in the *Manchester Guardian*, on which I have freely drawn for the Bhoodan, East Wind–West Wind, and Minorities chapters.

I am grateful to Mr. William L. Holland for permission to use parts of my article on Nehruism which first appeared in the September 1955 issue of *Pacific Affairs* and to Mr. Geoffrey Crowther for permission to use some material on Gandhi and Gramdan which first appeared in *The Economist*.

I am grateful to Mr. Marcel Rodd for permission to use excerpts from Swami Probhavananda and Christopher Isherwood's translation of *Bhagavad-Gita*, published by Harper & Brothers and the New American Library of World Literature.

Finally, I am indebted to my husband for his infinite patience in putting at my disposal his eighteen years of experience in India and for his even more patient correcting of my spelling.

                                                          Taya Zinkin

CONTENTS

INTRODUCTION

Under the winds of change a land inhabited by 380 million people, one sixth of humanity, is waking up, stretching limbs stiffened with the slumber of centuries. In one sweep India is undergoing all the revolutions which have taken two centuries in the rest of the world. Equality and political rights; industrialization and urbanization; agrarian reforms and agricultural improvements; science and technology; social and personal emancipation are combining to transform a contented, static, rural, ritualistic society into a new and dynamic one where privilege is no longer inherited, where women are men's equals, and where Harijans (untouchables) are as important as Brahmins.

Originally Hindu society was divided into four castes and the outcastes. The four castes are, in order of decreasing status: Brahmins — priests and scholars; Kshatryas — soldiers and kings; Vaishyas — merchants and bankers; Sudras — cultivators and artisans. Below the Sudras there are the Harijans, who are the outcastes. Brahmins, Kshatryas, and Vaishyas wear the sacred thread, a sign of the status of their castes. The sacred thread is put on boys, at about the time they reach puberty; and is the outward symbol of the fact that they are 'twice born.' Being twice born merely means that one has been formally initiated into one's religious fold, much like a First Communion; the sacred thread is worn only by men.

This book is an attempt to show the many ways in which India is changing. These ways are so interwoven that it is impossible to say where one change ends and the next begins. How is one to draw the line between individual and social change? between political and economic change? Especially when the political changes are so smooth as to be, sometimes, almost imperceptible.

The changes are all embracing and take many forms in a country as vast and diverse as India, where what is true for one area need not be true for another, where customs vary not only from village to village but from sub-caste to sub-caste. Beyond the simple assertion that India is changing it is impossible to be dogmatic.

Westerners tend to think of India as a land of child-marriages, eternal widowhood, joint-families, and vegetarianism; this is because intimate contact between Indians and foreigners was largely confined to the educated upper castes, one sixth of the population or less. The majority, however, marry in their late teens, divorce, remarry, eat meat, and set up individual households. And, as India becomes modern, the old Hindu ways are gradually loosening their hold even on the top castes. Change has not yet done more than shake India's stability, a stability which comes from the comforting warmth of its village life, a warmth which will disappear as India is transformed from a backward peasant country into a modern nation.

This book about a generation in transition is largely based on personal observation. Almost every book about India must be so in the absence of adequate information. Even if statistical data were available it could not describe India's transformation. One has to rely very largely on what one has seen oneself, or on what one has been told by others who have seen themselves. Inevitably some of one's conclusions will be unwarranted, or distorted, or incomplete. For such mistakes I can only apologize in advance.

Taya Zinkin

Bombay
15 *January* 1958

PART ONE 🙰 INDIA AS IT WAS

The Indian Village

There is no such thing as a typical Indian village. In India there are over 558,000 villages, and they vary astonishingly from area to area. There are the smoky, filthy pigsties on stilts in which the Naga head-hunters of Assam live; the prow-shaped, thatched Toda villages of Madras; the mud-walled fortresses of the Punjab; the rural cities of Gujerat, with their hundred-thousand-dollar, three-story mansions; the Ladakhi hill-cut houses, strangely akin to the creations of Frank Lloyd Wright; the houseboats of Kashmir with their floating vegetable gardens; the palm-matted bashas of Bengal; the neat little wooden houses of Travancore-Cochin; the scattered huts of the coast of Malabar; and the painted villages of Rajasthan, where charging elephants trample over sleeping lions and the blue smoke of prehistoric railway engines coats the mud walls.

In some villages, the houses have straw roofs; in others, the roofs are corrugated iron sheets; elsewhere again they are made of cool Mangalore tiles, raw mud bricks, or bamboo tubes. Some houses are huts with only one room; others are a maze of structures, with courtyard following courtyard and roof overlapping roof in unending succession. In Saurashtra, animals get pride of place in the inner courtyard, in front of the living room, next to the kitchen. Elsewhere, animals are housed on the ground floor, below their owners, or even

are kept on rafters overhead. In some villages, the hearth is in
the one room where people sit, eat, sleep, and keep stores; in
many others, the hearth is outside, in the open, by the stack
of cow-dung cakes.

By and large, Indian villages fall into two categories:
Northern villages and Southern villages. The majority are
nucleated villages, with the houses gathered close together,
but dispersed villages are an exception dear to the hearts of
individualistic aboriginals and the Indians of the coconut
country in the far Southwest. Southern villages are, on the
whole, clean and pleasant. Northern villages, which the hasty
tourist sees because they are around Delhi and the Taj Mahal,
are nearly always dirty and rarely pleasant, though some are
prosperous. Yet, North or South, Telugu or Punjabi, Mahratta
or Assamese, Hindu or Moslem, all Indian villages have certain features in common.

Indian villages have no shape; they are not picturesque like
French villages, which cluster around a château or a church.
India has had little feudalism in the Western sense and, since
Hinduism has no real congregational worship, there is no
great need for temples. Many villages do have temples, but
few of them are well kept and some are mere shacks. There
are of course a few magnificent and elaborate temples. These
were built by kings as an expression of their faith or, as in
Malabar, by the landed rich who wanted temples of their
own to avoid hobnobbing with all and sundry in the house
of the Lord. Even where there are temples in India, villages
do not cluster around them, in the way they do around
churches in the West.

As a rule, an Indian village presents no center of worship
to the foreigner's eye. This is an illusion. An Indian village
really swarms with temples of all kinds — important temples,
small temples, old temples, new temples. To discover them,
the foreigner must have the diviner's gift for detecting the
hidden. How could he guess that the two bricks, smeared with
cow dung, against the stump of the tree behind the hut on

the right-hand side of the road, are the much-revered temple of a local godling who makes women bear sons and protects the village — all its castes, from top to bottom — from smallpox? Or that the stone at the entrance of the village is worshiped by the people in the neighboring houses? The stone looks like any old stone, greasy on top, with a few withered marigold petals scattered on the dust around it. The Westerner, accustomed to churches with a recognizable structure, has no way of guessing what every Indian infant knows: God is everywhere — in the stone, in the peepul tree, in the dung of the cow. It does not matter how, where, or under what name He is worshiped as long as His existence is remembered.

An Indian friend of mine in the Forest Department once complained bitterly that in his subdivision he had great difficulty shifting a boundary mark. The mark was a stone painted red, to which the villagers of the surrounding hills were in the habit of offering flowers and food. It did no good to tell them that the stone was only a landmark of the Forest Department. Each time the officer's men moved the boundary mark they ran grave risks from protesting villagers.

Indian villages are not planned. They spread jaggedly into their own fields as the population grows. That is why their houses straggle down a long main street instead of circling around the well, which is the heart of the village. Indeed, though it may be half a mile or more from the newest house, the well is to an Indian village what the village green is to an English village.

Indian villages are not beautiful, except for those on the West Coast and in Rajasthan. They have no shaded alleys. The houses encroach messily on each other and on the gutters which serve as streets. There are neither flowers nor public gardens; at best, the lone blob of green of a papaya tree, sticking up in a corner next to a rubbish heap, relieves the monotony. There is no sewage system, not even a trench latrine, and refuse is often dumped on the path, right in front of the house. In Rajasthan, flayed carcasses sometimes rot in the

village itself; nobody seems to mind. In Northern India, even
the sewage pits of individual houses may overflow into the
street, vomiting their stench and germs to the delight of flies,
pie dogs, and rats.

Many villages are in urgent need of repair. They are as
messy and dirty as backward Savoy villages, but lack their
solidity, because in India durable construction materials such
as brick, stone, or hard wood have, in most areas, been reserved for temples and palaces. That is why the Indian village
is not old; its decrepitude is not because of its years but the
junkiness of its building materials, the rigor of the climate,
and the lack of skill of its masons. There are exceptions, of
course, such as the houses of peasant landlords in Gujerat
and Malabar, but on the whole, village houses are built of
junk.

Indeed, the only thing an Indian village has in common
with an American village or town is its comparative newness.
The oldest house in a Gujerat village, where they often build
in stone, will be perhaps one hundred and fifty years old and
an object of great local pride because of its age.

Many of the houses beyond repair have been abandoned
haphazardly in mid-village, to the delight of children who use
them for games of hide-and-seek and slide-down-my-bottom.
They also serve the men, who have in them facilities of an
almost French ubiquity but with more privacy. Such conven-
iences are necessary, for the Indian village has no toilet facilities — a situation that the Community Projects are only beginning to change.

As a rule, there are no roads, drains, or lavatories (public
or private); also there is normally no running water. No matter how prosperous it is, every household has to get its water
from a well — which is often between twenty and seventy
feet deep — in buckets or jars. This means an endless trek
for the women, to and fro through mud and dirt between
their house and the well — unless they have a well in their
courtyard. Even carrying three copper pots at a time on her

head, a woman may make many trips to provide the day's water for her household.

The Indian village has none of the community life that centers around the castle, the church, or the bakery in Europe, or around the drug store in America. Nor does an outsider immediately see any signs of trade. Small villages have no shop at all, and only big villages have a store. Often the only place for trade is a few stalls or a local weekly market. There is no Main Street, no shopping center. Most villagers trade at market places or with itinerant vendors who amble along with their wares — glass bangles, plastic toys or combs, colored lithographs, glass beads, bright ribbons, and pocket mirrors — dangling from trays precariously suspended around their waists. In the dingy stall of the merchant the villager may buy rusty nails, indigenous cigarettes rolled in tree leaves, stale cigarettes in packets of ten, grains, pulses, and spices in little mounds of color, betel nuts and pan leaves (India's pungent chewing gum), coarse salt, cheap mill-made cloth, kerosene and cooking oil in dirty bottles, soap, and matches — but little else. For the rest, either the villager is self-sufficient or he goes to market once a month in the nearest big village, which is perhaps a mile away across plowed fields. However, the mud track, which is the main 'road,' may well snake along two or three miles before reaching it.

The things the villager does regularly in the village — such as getting a shave, having his plow repaired, or buying a pot — are most likely paid for in kind after the harvest. If he needs money he has no bank to approach about a loan; he borrows from his better-off neighbor or from a moneylender, who is a merchant or a rich peasant.

The village has no movie house, no hotel, no restaurant, and no railroad station. It has no amenities in the Western sense, and a foreigner in an Indian village is entirely at the mercy of local hospitality for even a drop of water or a place to sit down. Nowadays the Indian village has a school. Bigger villages have a post office, and many smaller ones have a letter

box. If a village is really big, it will have a radio set and it
may have a dispensary or a weekly fair or a whole street of
shops.

The villager is not wholly cut off from the world. He makes
an occasional visit to the local *tetsil* (county) town to sell his
crops, and while there he listens to a newspaper being read
aloud or goes to a movie. Perhaps he enjoys the movies so
much because he goes only once in three months. At home
he must rely on wandering minstrels, beggars, neighbors' disputes, and family ceremonies to keep him amused.

It is easy to see why outsiders who do not know them might
consider Indian villages squalid beyond words, poor beyond
despair. Yet, for those who know, it is a good place to live.
It has beauty, friendliness and fun, an organization of its own
and a place for everybody.

The village may be dirty, but the people are clean and the
houses are swept. The average Indian bathes every day or
every other day, and, in the South, almost everyone washes
his clothes every day or, at the very least, twice a week. There
are exceptions, of course. In Rajasthan and Saurashtra, people
bathe only once a week or once a fortnight, while the Ladakhis
are bathed only twice in a lifetime: when they are born and
before they are cremated. Because soap is new and not yet
fully accepted, many people bathe with plain water, gram
flour, pumice stone, mud, or soap nut; they save soap for
ceremonial occasions.

As for the houses, they are swept at least once a day with
a broom made of sticks. This is a less efficient tool than a
vacuum cleaner, for it only displaces dust, but it leaves few
cobwebs. Every day the kitchen floor is smeared with a
mixture of mud, water, and cow dung, whose very real antiseptic properties are appreciated in India as they are not in the
West. The cooking vessels, too, are spotless, although they
are cleaned with ashes or mud. The Pasteurian revolution has
not yet reached India.

To an outsider the village looks formless — not so to the

initiated. The street — that dawdling foot path which zigzags haphazardly from one rubbish heap to the next — has a rigorous organization. In one street live only the potters of the village. They may not all make pots, but they all belong to the potter caste. The Brahmins have their streets; the peasants, theirs. A bit of field separates the touchable village from the Harijan, or untouchable. The Harijans have the same rigid organization: the sweepers' street, the leatherworkers' street, and, far removed, the carrion-eating basket-weavers' street — the lowest of the low.

The village is organized in accordance with the implicit but formidable tradition of caste. A Brahmin cannot eat with a lower caste; a barber will not take water from a leatherworker; and a barber will feel free of pollution, whether he is polluting or being polluted, only in the company of another barber. It is, therefore, sensible to put likes together — not only to make eating and drinking easy, but also to reduce the snubs of a rigidly stratified world for a growing child.

This is not the only organization in the village. There is also organization within each house, camouflaged in a maze of inner and outer courtyards and sheds. The houses may follow a wavering building line and their walls may have cracks, but inside all is busy order. In one corner of the courtyard, the youngest child swings in a hammock in time with the rhythmic pounding of the grain. 'Hong ho' go the tall, polished wooden poles, which fall in perfect rhythm from the hands of the two women. The husk is tossed up from a deep hole as the bouncing beam is thrust down. 'Grum, grum' go the heavy stone wheels as, turned by the twist of an expert hand, they grind their rough surfaces together, spilling the nourishing dust of the flour around this homemade mill, ancient as civilization itself. In another corner, above the stacks of wooden implements — the hoe, the plow, the pitchfork — a patch of bright red peppers drying in the heat makes, with a lonely sunflower or a yellowy white cluster of frangipane, a cheerful dash of color.

Inside, the walls are decorated with tinsel, a peacock-feather fan, a beaded fringe, a gaudy one-cent colored lithograph of Mahatma Gandhi or Hanuman (the monkey god) or Krishna playing his flute. In an alcove, a shabby photograph of an ancestor, garlanded with dead marigolds, is safely locked in a hollow behind glass. And in the farthest corner of all, away from the light, there are jars of baked clay, dried mud, or matted bamboos, large enough to hide not only Ali Baba but also his forty thieves. The family savings are the grain and seed stored in these giant jars from year to year. The only other source of savings is the gold and silver ornaments which the women wear. Silver in crude but artistic designs drips from the necks, ankles, toes, arms, waists, ears, and even the noses and the hair of the younger women. Babies have silver belts around their naked bellies. The whole household jingles and tinkles to the song of its savings.

The house or hut is not comfortable. There is no furniture. There are, at most, the few nuptial trunks in which the dowry came and which are now kept under a string cot. Most people sleep on the ground or on matting; the string cot is for the sick or to sit on in the shade during the day. Vegetables that are drying for storage, or anything that must be kept safe from ants and mud, may be on the cot.

The individuality of each home comes from the earth-colored frescoes so frequently painted on its mud walls. An airplane, childish in outline, outmoded in design, perilously tilts its nose next to a window; or a bird on a twig cheers up the main wall. At times the patterns are geometric, if only the repetition of tapering fingers, fanwise around the walls, at eye level. The ingenuity of the women is never exhausted. They spend hours, indeed days, decorating the hut with their imaginative art.

Even the well, such a wearying distance from the hut, is a center of beauty when the women gather to gossip. There you can see the unerring beauty of the Indian color sense. Only a village lass would dare mix in her clothes the colors of Rouault, of Matisse, and of Marie Laurencin: a bright deep violet skirt; a lemon green scarf, fuschia dotted, with a hint of absinthe on maroon; gold or silver tinsel on the hem; and somewhere a shy, tender pink. The close-fitting brassiere is more daring still — black and burnt sienna, with a splash of azure, just on the tip. And below this Impressionist's rainbow is the lovely golden brown of a body that has never run to fat. Silver bells jingle around slim ankles, the sun glistens on the copper pots high on her head giving the appearance of a triple-tiered crown. Her hips sway, her head is erect, her body is straight with the straightness of a sugar cane; she treads barefoot with the bearing of a queen.

Beauty in an Indian village does not end with the women. There are the children, dark imps with huge, velvety eyes. And there is the damp muzzle of the new-born water-buffalo calf, licking a fly away with his pale blue tongue. In the distance are the creaking music of the bullock cart's wheels, the hunter's call of its driver, the colorful turbans of the men.

Life in the village is so warm and comfortable that the villager leaves it only when he is pushed by hunger or ambition. But, even if he becomes a big man in the city, he retains a deep loyalty for his village, for no success, however great, can re-create for him the warmth of belonging that he has left behind.

The Warmth of Belonging

In India, everybody belongs, in many ways and in many directions, to many groups. Nobody has to fight to get accepted; everybody *belongs* from birth. To belong is reassuring and warm — like being wrapped in a cocoon. This warmth of belonging, which exists from the first moment of consciousness, explains much of Indian psychology.

'Lorsque l'enfant paraît, le cercle de famille s'agrandit.' Victor Hugo might have had India in mind when he wrote this. India is perhaps the most reassuring place in the world for a child to grow up in. A child's life begins with the certainty of being wanted. 'Have you ever noticed,' ask many visiting sociologists, 'that Indian children, especially in the villages, never cry? Within their own society and their own caste they seem to have no complexes. They are among the world's happiest children, for they are truly loved by everyone.'

Indian children are loved and spoiled to a degree that no other children are. They may starve because their parents are poor; they may have rickets and feed on worms and slugs in times of famine; but they are never ignored or harshly treated. There is in India none of the Victorian belief that children should be seen and not heard. From birth to death, the Indian child — he may be grown up, but to his parents he is forever a child — is loved and coddled. Whenever he starts crying, his mother nurses him, his father leaves his work to carry him, his sister rocks him or, like Gulliver's Lilliputian mother, carries him astride her hip. Letting a child cry is to Indians as unthinkable as torturing a dog is to a member of the Society for the Prevention of Cruelty to Animals. Indeed, whenever I punished my son, my entire Indian household looked upon me as a beast: the cook wept, the butler suddenly became deaf to the bell in protest, and even the driver sulked in the garage.

The warmth of belonging follows the Indian throughout the whole of his life, for he belongs not only within his immediate family but also within his extended family, which spreads its web like a kindly spider. The seventh cousin of one's paternal great-uncle is as much a member of the family as one's own brother, and everyone has countless brothers and sisters. Within the family, the true Marxian creed is the rule: 'From each according to his means, to each according to his needs.' Even the imbecile brother must be provided with a wife and a home. This may be a terrible burden for the able-bodied, but it also means that nobody is cast out as unwanted. The specter of unemployment, disease, and old age is never as stark in India as it is in the highly competitive societies of the West. The family may quarrel — indeed, there is always quarreling, particularly among the women — but the family is there to protect the child, the adolescent, and the old against the hazards of fortune and the hostility of the outside world, for all are interdependent. This interdependence is most important in creating a sense of security in the individual, who may have only a few dealings with anyone not his kin.

There are many layers in village society — layers of age, family position, education, property, and caste — according to which an Indian has an inalienable position and within which he may become a person of importance and a leader.

Within the family itself, the individual's importance grows with age, for age is respected in India as success is in the United States. A man may be fifty years old and educated

far beyond his elders, but he still treats them with all the
respect due to age. He does not sit down or talk in front of
them without being invited to do so, and under no circumstances does he smoke in front of them. This respect for age
makes for contentment; it provides everybody with a place
within his own family. Thus, a government servant, holding
the position of a permanent Under-Secretary of State, will kiss
the feet of his village elders, if custom requires him to do so.
Traveled and educated though he may be, he will treat with
the utmost deference his great-uncle who may not even be
literate.

In the Delhi drawing room of a senior government official
it is not uncommon to find a country cousin — poor, semi-
literate, ill at ease with a fork, even unaccustomed to chairs.
The cousin is not a guest; the house is his by right of blood.
It never occurs to his host to hide him in a cupboard for poor
relations. If the poor cousin is older than his host, he gets
the place of honor at the head of the table, and the house is
run in accordance with his custom. During his visit, Westernized dishes like eggs or meat, Westernized gadgets like
plates and forks, are given up; and the whole family reverts to
a vegetarian diet which they eat from trays with their fingers.
Indeed, the host may sneak away like a schoolboy for a smoke.
If the poor relation has peculiar ideas, they must be indulged.
Pandit Nehru, the Prime Minister of India, had a great-aunt
who used to visit him once a year. On arrival, she would turn
every piece of furniture out of her room, wash the walls and
the floor herself with a disinfectant concoction of her own,
unpack her own cooking pots, and cook in her room on a
charcoal fire. She did not trust her great-nephew to observe
all the musts of his caste — and quite rightly, for Nehru has
always had a Harijan as a cook.

In India, social position depends not on success alone but
on one's original position in one's family and village. For
example, my Scottish friend Jim's experience could have happened only in India. Jim was in the Indian Civil Service be-

fore Independence. Shortly before Independence he began to make arrangements to leave, to the sorrow of his faithful valet, Somia, a Harijan from Bihar. One day Somia said to Jim: 'Sahib, don't go. You are needed in India. I promise you that you will get a good job if you stay. Yesterday I had dinner with my "little brother," and when I told him that my Sahib is going and what a good Sahib too, Jagjivan told me to tell you from him to stay.'

Somia's friend Jagjivan was none other than the Union Minister for Labour, Sri Jagjivan Ram, a Harijan from Somia's village. Despite his education and his long political career, he and Somia had preserved unchanged the relationship of their youth when they played together around the village well. When Somia went to dinner with the Minister, it was the valet who did the Minister an honor because the valet was older.

Education is highly valued in India, and as long as the young remember to treat their elders with all due deference, they are listened to with a respect they can never command in the West, where almost everyone can read. The child who makes up his father's accounts, the young high-school graduate who reads the newspaper aloud to the village elders, and the schoolteacher who reads the village records, explains official announcements, and acts as the village scribe — all are respected for their learning.

Position depends also on possessions. It is natural for a rich peasant to be respected. Much of the village economy depends upon his initiative. He alone can start a new crop, for he alone has spare land to risk. He employs others. He contributes to the upkeep of the temple and distributes sweetmeats to the priests and the beggars at festivals. His status is raised further still when he entertains visiting officials and ministers, for his is the only big house. To receive a government official or a party boss means a lot in a world where the traditional respect for government is as deep rooted as it is in India. (This respect for government is traditional, for government not only maintains law and order but it provides water to much of India by means of irrigation.) Moreover, when it comes to building a well for the village, a school, or a pilgrim's hostel, the richer peasant donates money and sometimes even land.

Everybody in India is born into and belongs to a particular caste and subcaste. Caste may be the curse of Indian society, but it is also the safeguard of the individual. Within his caste, nobody is lonely and anybody can become a leader.

Caste makes a honeycomb of the Indian village, the cells hermetically sealed from each other, yet, as in a beehive, absolutely interdependent. The Brahmin would starve if he were not fed by the farmer. The farmer would be poisoned if he did not have a Harijan to remove carcasses and to clean gutters and wells. The Harijan would die of thirst and hunger if a caste villager did not draw water for him from the well or employ him on his lands.

The caste division of labor is somewhat similar in its practice to that of the labor unions of the West, which forbids an electrician to mend a tap. Indeed, in the beginning — three thousand years ago in Vedic times — caste may have been merely an occupational division. The blacksmith taught his son to work metal, just as the Brahmin taught his son the Vedas. There was then no rigid barrier between the castes. Many a Brahmin began life as a warrior. But gradually caste became hereditary. Even then, there were no restrictions on intercaste marriages: the demi-gods of the *Mahabharata* — at once the *Iliad* and the Bible of Hinduism — could be sons of warrior kings and fisherwomen. However, since only the Brahmins and the twice born were permitted to read the Vedas, they began to exploit caste for their own ends. Yet, for quite some time, no stigma was attached to untouchability.

Oppression of the untouchables always has had its limits. The Harijan may be poor and illiterate, but he holds the village at his mercy. Whenever Harijans have gone on strike, they have won because they are indispensable. That is why even at the height of a water famine, Harijans are still given drinking water by their neighbors, who know that if, by the time the rains come, all the Harijans have died or migrated in search of water, there will be nobody to do the plowing.

Happiness, like poverty, is relative. A Harijan may be desperately poor, but he matters within his own little world; he can even one day be an elder, respected by his fellows for his white hair. Even his world spills over into the larger world of the village in the circles he knows. Furthermore, a young Harijan with a scholarship can aspire to lead the whole village with the special skills he acquires at school.

By leaving his native village to work in a factory at Calcutta or Bombay, an Indian may escape the bonds of caste and possibly achieve complete equality, but in so doing he discards the warm and comforting security of his village for the hostile world of equal competition. In the city, if he is lame, lazy, stupid, old, or ill, he sinks to the gutter; if he is bright and industrious, he rises. But he can never be sure of re-creating around him the atmosphere of contentment into which he was born.

Along with the cocoon of environment, there are a number of outlets in Indian social organization through which an individual Indian may develop his personality. These outlets add considerably to the stability of society and to the happiness of the individual, and at the same time insure that the cocoon does not become so stifling that it must be slashed open. The outlets are the various councils that preside over village life: the Panchayats. The Panchayats are elected or nominated bodies with specific functions. There are two types: the caste Panchayat and the village Panchayat. The caste Panchayat is more often than not an instrument of regression while the village Panchayat, properly used, is an instrument of progress.

The purpose of the caste Panchayat is to preserve caste, subcaste, and custom in their pristine rigidity. (The Harijan castes have their own Panchayats.) The caste Panchayat decides what can and what cannot be done within the caste. It was the Panchayat of his caste that excommunicated Mahatma Gandhi for crossing the ocean to study law in Britain. The caste Panchayat lays down rules for marriage between distant relatives. It arbitrates family disputes and decides on the procedure for common-law marriage and common-law divorce. The caste Panchayat is usually composed of the oldest and most orthodox members of the caste; and elders, in a changing age, always tend to be unchanging.

Bad though some of its features may be, the caste Panchayat has its good points. It provides the members of the caste with the equivalent of a parish fund. If a man dies away from home, it will provide free the necessary mourners, the money for the funeral, and the corpse bearers. It may also provide interest-free loans for education or business. Properly used, it can be a powerful weapon in support of social claims, for it has great authority in rural areas where few people are educated. If a caste Panchayat orders the boycott of another caste in a fight for 'fairer wages,' it will be obeyed by the entire caste as no union leader would be. But, with the spread of education and increased urbanization, its power is gradually declining.

The ancient institution of the village Panchayat is truly a council of elders. It was once so powerful that it merited this description from Sir Charles Metcalfe in 1832:

The village communities are little republics, having nearly everything they want within themselves, and almost independent of any foreign relations. They seem to last where nothing else lasts. Dynasty after dynasty tumbles down; revolution succeeds revolution . . . but the village community remains the same . . . This union of village communities, each one forming a separate little state in itself, has, I conceive, contributed more than any other cause to the preservation of the people of India, through all the revolutions and changes which they have suffered, and is in a high degree conducive to their happiness, and to the enjoyment of a great portion of freedom and independence.

This was primarily the case in those areas where kingly authority was remote, fitful, and, at best, concerned only with the levying of taxes. Everything had to be done by the village for itself.

With the firm establishment of British rule later in the nineteenth century, however, the village Panchayats wilted and the villagers became apathetic, less willing to help themselves, and dependent on the Government for almost everything. This was a mixed blessing for England, for, while it made revolt slower, it made progress slower, too. By the early 1930's, the British in India realized that, in the long run, progress in the village was more important than apathy. In their attempt to repair the damage, they revived village Panchayats on an elective basis. Their efforts were soon frustrated, however, when the Congress Movement forced them to divert their attention from social rehabilitation to keeping law and order. This is why today the village Panchayats need many vitamins if they are to become useful again.

The State Governments of India have made a considerable effort to provide these vitamins, for the Panchayats are one of the channels through which they are trying to reach the villagers in their program of rural development. The village Panchayats have been vested with functions similar to those of a municipal council; in some States, they even collect land revenue on behalf of the Government for a commission; elsewhere, they may merely decide the location of a new school or whether to repair an approach road. The new village Panchayats have succeeded in many places: in Uttar Pradesh, for instance, they have kept tens of thousands of cases out of the courts. They have also often failed. To the Government's distress, they have often proved to be socially retrograde and anything but democratic. The members, who are frequently elected according to caste rather than to competence, may use their office to serve the ends of their own caste rather than those of the village community. Panchayat elections may exacerbate, rather than heal, village factions.

On the other hand, in Uttar Pradesh there are a few cases where Harijans are secretaries of village Panchayats. In Saurashtra, the Government is trying to make the institution a solvent of untouchability by refusing to register Panchayats that do not have Harijan members. Finally, the breakdown of hereditary office-holding and the restrictions that the State governments have placed upon the amount of land an individual may own can act to make the village Panchayat a more democratic and, therefore, more effective instrument.

Besides the caste and the village Panchayats, there is an admirable but dying institution: the caste courts. These courts are made up of respected elders of the village: in the South, they are often Brahmins; in the West, often farmers; in the North, warriors. These elders know everybody, they are respected by all, and they are ideal dispersers of justice, Solomon-wise. Their age gives weight to their judgment; their reputation has to be preserved; they are not influenced by money or kinship. Therefore, they judge intercaste quarrels, as well as quarrels between members of a caste lower than their own. Because they belong to a village — and in a village everybody knows everything about everyone — their verdict is more in keeping with justice than that of a government court at the district headquarters, where the judges know nothing of local circumstances. A good example of the injustice of headquarters justice happened to my husband, a member of India's Civil Service until 1947:

'When justice is removed from the place of the conflict, justice is often more than just blind; it can be unjust in the extreme. There was the case of a villager whose new house, two stories high, was encroaching on a road. My order was summary: pull the wall down. Roads are public property and encroachments cannot be tolerated. The villager wrote back in protest: he was not encroaching and the government was not being fair. The case dragged on for two years until I happened to pass through that village. The culprit begged me to come and see for myself if he was encroaching or not. His house, a magnificent village building, stood at the end of the village, on a cul-de-sac road which served only his house. I learned a great lesson there and then: always go and see for yourself.'

Caste courts were best suited for the isolated villages of old, though now, with increasing State interference and the spread of communications, they are dying away.

The most compelling reason why the villager looks on his village as his kingdom and on his hut as his castle is probably the fact that the poorest of the poor, the lowest of the Harijans, the most miserable of human beings is still almost everywhere in India the owner of his house. The house may be only a hovel of rags, cans, and straw, fit perhaps for a dog, but it is the villager's own. The cans, the rags, the straw belong to him and, although the land may not, he knows he will not be evicted and that his children will live on the same spot after him. It is one of the miracles of India that, except in the towns, everybody owns his own roof. There are no village tenements for hire, no equivalent to the farm hand being chucked out of the loft where he has been living during his employment, or — as in France — being repatriated to Italy or North Africa after the harvest. Even plantation laborers, who are housed with their families on a plantation, have their ancestral roof back in their jungles. The landless laborers who go to Calcutta to work in jute mills or to Bombay to work in textile mills all have a wife and a hut of their own back home. The wife may starve, the hut may be perched on an uninviting site, but both are inalienably his. This fact has great implications in the political and economic life of India: it explains the laborer's reluctance to move and it provides a continuing reason for him to return to his village. And with each return come new ideas, thus lessening the isolation of the village.

The most reassuring aspect of an Indian's life may well be the intimacy of his relations with God and the informality of his faith. Although it has both, Hinduism needs no tem-

ples, no priests. Except for such ceremonies as marriage, every
Hindu is his own priest. Hinduism is in one sense a religion
of the home. Each household has its own god, like the Roman
lares and penates, presiding over the day-long chores of the
womenfolk from his little niche by the entrance to the
kitchen. His is an honored position and he is the friend of all,
from the children who love the tinsel and the saffron on his
plaster forehead, to the women who make of him a real friend
and confidant. And although the men may not pay their
respects to their home god every day, they never fail to show
their respect by devotions at festival times in the prescribed
manner. In the hut, the god is poor but loved. All that is
good goes to his credit; all that is bad is told him many times
over, with that affectionate reproof a mother has for a
naughty child. And since the relationship is intimate in the
extreme, if God fails to oblige, he can be abused, threatened,
even punished. The family god has a birthday, when he is
washed, garlanded, and fed his favorite sweetmeat. He has
his holidays, his weekly feast day. He is more than a god and
a friend; he is a member of the household. A friend, yet a
God. How soothing to the children sleeping in the dark! How
precious to the girl who prays for a husband as handsome as
Krishna, as powerful as Siva! How comforting to the wife
sorrowing over the health of her young or the death of a bullock! Because in the West our relations with God are formal,
because we go to His house to pray, we cannot know how it
feels to have God around all the time, in the kitchen and
the living room, a pensioner in the house. Many an Indian
widow devotes the rest of her life to her kitchen god, earning
the respect of the village — for does she not prepare sweets
for the little god every day, does she not wash his feet and
change his clothes and chant songs to put him to sleep and
fan him in the hot afternoons, leaving the care of her own
life to village charity or to her respectful children? Ganesh
may be fat, made of clay, and a trifle gaudy, but he has filled

with forgetfulness the desert of one life, and after all Ganesh is but another name for God.

Besides the kitchen god in every hut, the village is full of deities. Each one comes to life to the tinkle of bells and the smell of offerings on the particular day when it is his turn to be honored. Knowing the gods is half the fun of a villager's life, for, besides births, weddings, and funerals, where would the excitement come from if not from religious festivals? Religious festivals are very important in India, for not only do they provide the village with entertainment, piety, and reassurance against evil but they are the occasion on which each caste asserts its place in the hierarchy of society, while at the same time the village as a whole asserts its unity. A festival is of interest to all castes, whether they participate or watch.

The festivals vary from one part of India to another. In the South, the Festival of Cattle celebrates the harvest, for which man and beast must work together with all speed before the coming of the rains. For a brief time, the bulls, the cows, and the bullocks become the center of the villagers' attention. They are well fed, well washed, and decorated with garlands of auspicious flowers; their horns are painted a luscious gold, red, deep blue, or saffron, with tassels and bells strung to their tips.

In Northern, Eastern, and Central India, villagers observe Holi, a festival to welcome spring. The main feature of the festival is the sprinkling of colored water on one another. Holi is perhaps the most boisterous and noisy of all the festivals, the one that begins well and ends sadly. Caste, social position, age, all differences are forgotten for twenty-four hours, while children and rowdies, drunk with their short-lived equality, make a nuisance of themselves. Firecrackers go off, and everyone — the President of India, the Prime Minister, the village elder — gets his share of watery dye. Holi is fun but, like a *corrida*, it leaves scars. A villager's only shirt and dhoti will never recover from the red, blue, and saffron

stains, which may fade in time but will never quite wash
away. The infectious gaiety, begun in good faith, may end in
tears, sometimes in death. Old hostilities revive, as in the
village in Uttar Pradesh, where the objections of one section
of the village to being sprayed by another section ended with
the spiking to death of an entire family. In Bengal, Holi begins with fraternization between Moslems and Hindus, but
it sometimes ends in small communal riots. Yet every year,
despite it all, the Indian villager stocks up on colored powders
and recklessly ruins his neighbors' clothes. Perhaps it is the
safety valve for an otherwise placid people.

Then there is Divali, the finest of all festivals and certainly
the one to which the children look forward most. Divali celebrates the triumph of Good over Evil, of Light over Darkness. Relatives, friends, and neighbors give each other syrupy
sweets and set off fireworks and firecrackers. There is much
noise of the Fourth of July kind, but the spirit is quite different: it is one of fun and beauty. From dawn, the women
prepare thousands of little clay lamps — the same as in the
days of Pompeii — fill them with oil and a cotton wick, and
place them around the house at regular intervals — on the
roof, the window frame, the veranda, by the path, along the
street, and around the well. Even the poorest have their oil
lamps. The moment the sun sets that evening, little stars
light up the dark, lending to the most squalid village a glory
and a beauty of its own. There is something quiet and har-
monious in the burning of an oil wick in a little pot of clay,
something neon signs and electric lights cannot match: there
is peace.

There are also various seasonal festivals — sowing; harvesting; the mid-monsoon, when coconuts are thrown into the
sea; the meeting of two auspicious stars on their celestial
round, when one must bathe away one's sins in the river.
There are religious festivals, where the initiative comes from
the temples and the ritual from the people. These festivals
have a certain competitive spirit and are reminiscent of Span-

ish *romerías*, when an entire village or a number of villages join in one procession. In the East and in Mysore there is Durga Puja, the worship of the Goddess of Death. In Bombay there is Ganapathi Puja, the worship of the elephant-headed god who removes obstacles from one's path. In Orissa there is the giant festival of God Jagannath, the Unfinished, the elemental god whose chariot is pulled by thousands of devotees. In Delhi, at Ramlila, giant effigies of the evil Rawana demon are burned in public after they have been defeated by the hero Rama, India's model of virtue.

All the festivals have certain factors in common. The deity is always taken in procession to its grave 'so that people, once they have been reminded of the existence of God, should not confuse the image with the principle' — as our young son once explained. The procession may take as long as eight days to cover a few yards. It is punctuated with singing, the clanging of cymbals, the eating of sweetmeats, dancing, and good fun.

There are great pilgrimages on auspicious occasions, when millions of people trek across India to bathe in the sacred river Ganga on a given day. In 1953 perhaps twenty million came to the Kumbh Mela at Allahabad to immerse themselves at the confluence of the Jamuna and the Ganga.

These festivals, together with the many others added to the family festivals, marriages, births, and deaths — which are celebrated by gathering together and feeding relatives — provide the villager with plenty of opportunity to make merry.

To the warmth of belonging Indian society owes its great stability and its ability to act as a buffer. Its very stability, however, makes progress slow and difficult. For many years, there have been too many people on the land; yet it has never been easy to recruit labor in the towns. I have seen the half-famished villagers of Rayalaseema in South India prefer to starve on government gruel (550 calories) rather than move some sixty miles to earn their keep at the great dam then being built on the Tungabhadra.

Europe's larger industrial cities and the whole United States owe their existence to the fact that most village society in the West long ago lost its close-knit texture, in which everyone, however poor, had a warm and comfortable place and to which everyone felt he belonged. In the middle of the nineteenth century, the landless Western laborer left for the towns or for the New World. In either case, the excess population left the land and was drastically transformed. There is virtually nothing in common remaining between a third-generation American and his Irish or Italian cousin.

This is not true of the Indian who leaves his village. When he migrates to the city, to Ceylon, or to Malaya, he takes with him the 'air and water' of his village. He does not adapt; he clings to his food, dress, customs, language, and friends. (This is perhaps unavoidable since he still must find a husband for his daughter from his own people.) The chief complaint of the Singhalese, Burmese, Malays, or Africans is that Indians always remain Indians and keep to themselves in an Indian atmosphere which excludes the outsider. Although this is so partly because it makes arranging marriages easier, it is also because the Indian was so happy in his home and his village that he naturally tries to re-create around him the warmth of his early days.

※3※

Hinduism

All the current changes in Indian society take place within the double framework of Hinduism and that pragmatic liberalism which is the legacy of Gandhi.

Hinduism is infinitely flexible, infinitely difficult to define. A Hindu is born Hindu. One cannot normally become a Hindu. One cannot cease to be a Hindu; there is no excommunication, only social boycott. Hinduism has no official creed. Gandhi once wrote about Hinduism: 'A man may not believe even in God and still call himself a Hindu.' The essense of Hinduism is found in the Bhagavad-Gita (The Song of God, translated by Swami Prabhavananda and Christopher Isherwood):

> The ignorant work
> For the fruit of their action:
> The wise must work also
> Without desire
> Pointing man's feet
> To the path of his duty.

'You have the right to work, but for the work's sake only. You have no right to the fruits of the work. Desire for the fruits of work must never be your motive in working. . . . Renounce attachment to the fruits. . . . They who work selfishly for the results are miserable.' Duty without hope of reward is the key commandment of the Hindu scriptures.

The reward for doing one's duty, obediently and dispas-
sionately, is escape from the chain of rebirths. Thus, by losing one's ego one can free oneself from the bondage of virtue
and vice during this life. 'In the calm of self-surrender, the
seers renounce the fruits of their actions, and so reach enlightenment.' Then, 'free from the bondage of rebirth, they pass
to that state which is beyond all evil. . . . Death is certain
for the born. Rebirth is certain for the dead. You should not
grieve for what is unavoidable. . . . He Who dwells within
all living bodies remains forever indestructible. Therefore,
you should never mourn for anyone.'

The concept of doing one's duty is very rigid. The duty of
a soldier is to be a soldier, not a poet. Although one is *born* a
soldier, one does not necessarily have the soul of a soldier. A
soldier who has the soul of a priest must give up arms and
take up priesthood in order to be true to his duty. On this
the Gita is very clear. But it is equally clear that, if one is a
soldier, one must fight even if relatives and friends are on the
other side. 'To a warrior, there is nothing nobler than a right-
eous war. Happy are the warriors to whom a battle such as
this comes: it opens a door to heaven. . . . It is better to
do your own duty, however imperfectly, than to assume the
duties of another person, however successfully.'

The nature of man according to the Gita is not very different from the Carthesian definition. 'The nature of the individual man is his consciousness of ego,' say the Hindus.
'Cogito ergo sum,' wrote Descartes. The place of man in the
universe in terms of predestined duties is not so different in
the Hindu and the Jansenist traditions. The only difference
is that the Hindus emphatically believe that, since the will of
God cannot be anticipated, except by God himself, man remains free to choose; thus, his are the merits and the sins.

The Gita defines God thus:

Brahman is that which is immutable, and independent of any
cause but Itself. . . . The creative energy of Brahman is that
which causes all existences to come into being. . . . I alone am

God who presides over action, here in this body. . . . Therefore you must remember me at all times, and do your duty. . . . But behind the manifest and unmanifest, there is another Existence, which is eternal and changeless. . . . To reach it is said to be the greatest of all achievements. . . . Those who reach it are not re-born. . . .

Although I am not within any creature, all creatures exist within me. I do not mean that they exist within me physically. That is my divine mystery. My Being sustains all creatures and brings them to birth, but has no physical contact with them.

> For, as the vast air, wandering world-wide,
> Remains within the ether always,
> So these, my wandering creatures,
> Are always within me.
> . . .
>
> How shall these acts bind me, who am indifferent
> To the fruit they bear? For my spirit
> Stands apart, watching over
> Maya, the maker.
>
> Maya makes all things: what moves, what is unmoving.
> . . . that is why the world spins,
> Turning its wheel through birth
> And through destruction.
> . . .
>
> Great in soul are they who become what is godlike:
> They alone know me, the origin, the deathless:
> They offer me the homage
> Of an unwavering mind.

God is good, patient, forgiving: He gives man countless chances, He never rejects, nor is He exclusive in the imposition of His ways:

If a man will worship me, and meditate upon me with an undis-tracted mind, . . . I shall supply all his needs, . . . Even those who worship other deities, and sacrifice to them with faith in their hearts, are really worshipping me, . . . For I am the only enjoyer and the only God of all sacrifices. Nevertheless, such men must return to life on earth, because they do not recognize me in my

true nature. Those who sacrifice to the various deities, will go to
those deities . . . So, also, my devotees will come to me.

There are many ways to God in Hinduism. As the Gita
says, 'When the whole country is flooded, the reservoir becomes superfluous. So, to the illumined seer, the Vedas are
all superfluous.' For:

> The Lord is everywhere
> And always perfect:
> What does He care for man's sin
> Or the righteousness of man?

This is Hindu religion at its height. A religion without a
priesthood — 'To the illumined seer, the Vedas are all superfluous.' A religion with only one God — 'Some bow to the
countless gods that are only my million faces.' A religion
where the cycle of life is broken only when the itinerant has
reached eternity through perfection, a perfection of complete
renunciation and detachment by which he, no longer mortal,
having cleansed himself of all desire, is lost in God —

> The lotus leaf rests unwetted on water;
> He rests on action, untouched by action.

What does this sublime philosophy mean when it is translated into practice? It means perfect tolerance in the higher
religious sense. No Hindu dreams of converting a non-Hindu
to Hinduism. In a letter, a great Hindu scholar, Mr. C.
Rajagopalachari, revealed the extent to which a Hindu shrinks
from the slightest suggestion that a non-Hindu might look
to Hinduism as an answer:

. . . Your letters have confirmed my opinion that people should
not seek solace in religions that 'do not belong' to them. What
faith and ritual and traditions you are born and brought up in are
the best for your body and mental health. No one can get satisfaction or solace from Hinduism, unless he has been brought up in
the belief that souls do not expire when death happens. Infinite is
the length of days for each soul. Unless this has become as true as
the air you breathe, Hinduism will look and feel harsh and cruel
at all corners.

Further, in answer to a question of mine about the apparent injustice of the death of Bhishma, one of the heroes of the Mahabharata, Rajagopalachari pointed out:

Bhishma no doubt was killed, but that was a release, not a doom. Death came to him and brought Heaven with it. That is Hinduism. Bhishma had not the least notion that this life on earth ended his journey.

Hinduism is essentially monotheistic in spite of its many gods. The role of these gods in Hinduism is similar to that of the saints in the Roman Catholic Church. This monotheism was brought home to me one morning when my second house boy, Hari, came in with his forehead smeared with saffron powder and ashes. I asked him where he had been.

'To the temple to pray to Bhagvanji,' he answered. (Bhagvanji is the Hindu's generic term for God.)

'Which Bhagvanji?' I asked.

'Bhagvanji,' he replied, uncomprehendingly.

'I know, but which Bhagvanji? Hanuman? Siva? Parvati?' (Hanuman is the monkey god, Siva the destroyer, Parvati his wife.)

'Hanumanji,' he replied, 'but what does it matter? They are all the same. Siva, Parvati, Hanumanji — all of them are Bhagvanji.'

Like Roman mythology, Hinduism invited into its pantheon all the existing idols and symbols of the aboriginals, but it incorporated them as different aspects of a single, all-pervading God. The ancient Hindus took care to make this clear even in their sculpture, which shows the Oneness of God in its various manifestations. Thus, in the ancient rock temple at Ellora there are statues of half Siva-half Parvati, half Siva-half Vishnu, half Vishnu-half Brahma. And at Elephanta, near Bombay, the famous Trimurti (also known as the 'Maheshwamurti Siva') shows the three-headed deity in one: Brahma, the Creator; Vishnu, the Preserver; Siva, the Destroyer.

The common man's attitude to God was further clarified
for me when I visited Ellora. I chatted with one of the quite
illiterate guardians of this magnificent monument of man to
God. Commenting on the Siva Nataraja (a statue of Siva the
Destroyer, grief-stricken at Parvati's death, dancing the world
into destruction), I said, 'Isn't it terrible for Siva that his wife
should have died?'

The guardian looked at me with unconcealed contempt.
'But she is not dead. Siva *is* Parvati, and Siva is eternal. This
statue is merely a symbol of human fragility,' he said and
walked away in disgust.

As God has many forms, so God is everywhere. A truly
orthodox priest was once asked why the temple for which
he was responsible was so dilapidated and filthy. The Brahmin
answered frankly, 'It is just as well. A temple is merely stones.
God is everywhere.'

This sense of God's ubiquity is all-pervasive in India. It
even reached my six-year-old son, who laughed one day in
the middle of a spanking and said, 'Isn't God silly? Just fancy,
God beating himself! For there is just as much of God in
you as there is in me.'

I stopped, ashamed, while he went on, looking very superior. 'For that matter, there is as much of God in this chair
as there is in either of us.'

At about the same time, he explained Hinduism to a friend,
who had just come from England. The three of us had gone
to watch the Ganapati Puja on the Bombay beach. Ganapati
Puja is the occasion for the worship and ceremonial immersion of the elephant-headed god, Ganesha. My son's friend
was amazed at the noisy crowd and the sight of the elephant-
headed god decorated with garlands being dumped into the
sea.

'What is all this?' he asked.

Before I could answer, my son said, 'This is Ganapati Puja.
Ganesha is one of the Hindu gods. There are many others:
Jagannath, Durga, Siva, Krishna. These are all different names

for what we call God. Hindus remind themselves of the existence of God by building an image and praying to it for a
week. The praying is the puja. Then, to make sure that they
remember that this is not God, but only the image of God,
they destroy the clay image on the last day.'

In practice, the villager does not always remember what
the immersion ceremony is supposed to represent. He sometimes treats his image as if it were God. No matter what the
practice of the ignorant may be, however, deep down inside
all Hindus feel that God is one, that He is transcendent as
well as immanent, that he is universal.

This belief accounts for the deep reluctance of Hindus to
destroy any life. This reluctance is carried almost to absurdity
in a Jain sect, which holds life so dear that its devotees wear
a gauze mask on their faces so that they will not, even inad-
vertently, swallow insects. These same people walk with a
broom in their hands, sweeping the earth before them, in
order not to trample an ant (which may be the reincarnation
of a sinful mother-in-law). They eat only the leaves and
seeds of plants which have fallen to the ground. In areas of
Gujerat, where there are many such Jains, the Locust Control
Department has on occasion faced Jain riots because of its
efforts to exterminate locusts. During a famine, these Jains
feed cockroaches, ants, and other vermin, sometimes at the
expense of their own children. They may even lie on bug-
ridden beds purposely to feed these God-loved creatures with
their own blood. And when their flesh is too weak, they pay
a beggar a dollar a night to lie in for them.

The belief in the equality of man and beast is not confined
to Jains. Once as I was chatting with one of India's leading
politicians, a mosquito whizzed past. After I clapped it to
death, I said jokingly, 'I suppose you don't approve?'

'Frankly, no,' he answered. 'A mosquito is as much entitled
to live as a man. Of course, in my public capacity, I am responsible for the mass murder of millions of mosquitoes. [He
was referring to the extensive anti-malarial campaigns which

are being carried out successfully all over India.] One has to
dissociate one's responsibilities from one's private life. I must
confess, however, that I am still very far from having reached
Truth. I will not kill a mosquito, even if it bites me; but that
is not good enough. I should be able to love the mosquito
like my brother. And I can tell you that once I achieve this,
the mosquito will know it and won't bite me. For all creation
is responsive to love. Nobody who has loved a snake genuinely
has ever been bitten by it.'

'But surely if life was intended to be as nonviolent as all
this, man would not eat anything. Indeed, what would worms
feed on if they could not eat leaves?' I asked.

'Man should never eat life,' he replied. 'There are enough
fallen seeds and leaves for one's needs. Of course we do eat
many other things, but that is because we are weak. If we were
really strong, we could perfectly well eat nothing that is
alive, not even those seeds which are meant for germination.
And as far as worms are concerned, I have no doubt in my
mind that they could be trained, through love, not to eat
living leaves.'

This is both a Gandhian and a deeply Hindu way of looking at things. I once asked a well-known holy woman what
she thought of Hitler and how she reconciled his activities
with her philosophy. She does not speak English and she is
illiterate; yet she has a large following as a saint among some
of India's most distinguished intellectuals. She is a good,
kind-hearted, and loving person. Since she had never heard
of Hitler, I told her of the concentration camps he set up,
where innocent people were cold-bloodedly destroyed without
the excuse of either passion or self-defense. This was her response:

'If what you tell me is true, there are two points I wish to
make. One is that when you say that he is responsible for the
murder of millions of women and children, you forget that
with every breath of air you take, with every beat of your
heart, you are destroying living matter, millions of little germs

and cells. It is only human arrogance which makes us feel that these millions of inarticulate creatures of God are less important than the millions of Jews and Europeans you have spoken of.

'There is another way of looking at it. It is this. You do not know what thoughts were in Hitler's mind. So long as one does not know everything about a man, one cannot pass judgment, for there is good and bad in all of us. And who is to say which is greater in the eyes of God — an apparently very small good action or thought which has cost a great deal and was done or thought regardless of benefit, or a big wrong which may have been caused as part of one's place in the Wheel of Life? How do you know that Hitler was not merely the instrument of the will of God? Maybe his purpose was to liberate these people from past sins so that they could enter into a new and better life purified, not only by their sufferings, but by the way in which they bore their sufferings? It could be argued that Hitler was a great saint who broke his heart in doing his duty for the glory of God by taking upon himself the sin of being the instrument of his will.'

This incapacity to see a man or an action as all good or all bad, this constant giving of the benefit of the doubt, even to the Devil, is what makes for so much misunderstanding between India and the West. Hinduism is so all-embracing that Satan has a place in Heaven, too.

The essential features of Hinduism are not easily recognizable because, unlike the Judeo-Christian religions, Hinduism has not a set form of worship. It is so fluid in practice that it is impossible to define. A Hindu may eat beef, he may not believe in reincarnation, he may not believe in God — and he may still be a Hindu. The basic difference between Hinduism and the Judeo-Christian religions and Islam is that Hinduism is not a revealed, transmittable ethic, but an individual experience. It is an experience so unique that it can only be repeated by God-chosen individuals. These individuals — unlike Christian saints — influence the rest of society through their visual impact, rather than through their preaching. Their influence is felt by those chosen few who have had the good fortune to come into contact with these saints *after* they attained Brahma and *before* they died, and who in turn carry on the tradition through personal example.

Perhaps it is the apparent pantheism of Hinduism that makes it seem profane to many Westerners. The Moslems and the British used to condemn Hindus as 'idol-worshipers.' Even to this day, it is difficult for an intelligent and sympathetic Westerner with an Anglican background, for example, to feel immediately at ease with a Hindu, particularly if he sees one of the big festivals during his first few weeks in India. There is no doubt that the Hindu religion puts considerable emphasis on the outward trappings of faith in order to impress the worshiper with a healthy respect for God. The Roman Catholic Church does much the same thing and, indeed, it and Hinduism resemble one another in that they are highly formalistic. It is Protestants who, with their emphasis on austerity and abstract worship and their aversion to graven images, are repelled on their first experience of Hinduism. As is so often the case, first impressions are slow to disappear. Such was the case with the British in India. The failure of so many of them really to understand Hinduism was responsible for some of the worst of the errors in their treatment of India. This failure persists today. It has colored much Western thinking about India and has made it difficult for Westerners to understand the real problems and challenges of Indian society.

PART TWO 🙥 PERSONAL CHANGES

4

The Position of Women

The Indian woman occupies a God-given place in her society. She knows that place; yet in some cases she has attained spectacular emancipation without a struggle. For women in India have no need to fight for recognition; men are quite ready to make room for them. They do not face the male hostility that long made it difficult in America for a woman to become a successful doctor or lawyer.

Why is this so? The position of women in India stems from the place they occupy in Hindu mythology. There are no promiscuous Jupiters, no tempting Circes. Few are the escapades of the Hindu gods. Barring naughty little Krishna of the flute and his many milkmaids, the majority of the gods are not only married but very much at the beck and call of their wives. A goddess may, like Siva's wife, have many reincarnations, but she is always the same wife though her name may change with her mood. The great battle of Kurukshetra in the Mahabharata was fought, not so much because of the theft of the Pandava kingdom, but because the Kaurava kings tried to strip Draupadi, the Pandava wife. This is a sin that could only be washed out in the blood of battle, for is not 'the wife man's half? The wife is the first of friends. The wife is the root of Dharma, Artha, and Kama [human duty, wealth, and desire]. The wife is the root of Moksha [salvation]. A wife is the sacred field in which the husband is born himself.' *

Women are so respected in India that more than one foreign envoy has told me that it is one of the few countries where he does not worry if his young daughter travels alone. In India, it must be remembered, trains have no corridors. A young girl may be locked up between stations for hours at a time, sometimes for a whole night, in a compartment with a complete stranger. Sleeping compartments are mixed, and men do not take advantage of it to molest a woman.

Chivalry and respect for women are carried so far in India that an experience of mine during the general election of 1951 could, I think, have happened in no other country. At 4 a.m. one morning, I arrived in Kakinada, a little town in the rice-growing deltas of Madras, after twenty-four hours on a third-class passenger train. It had been an indescribable trip with no equivalent in modern Western life; I felt as though I was in the middle of Daumier's painting 'The Third-Class Carriage,' which lacks only the one hundred and fifty migrating professional beggars of my train. I was exhausted when I knocked at the door of the traveler's bungalow in Kakinada at dawn. My knock awoke a Union Minister who was occupying the only room and the only bed. He let me in and insisted that I take the bed; he would sleep on the porch. I insisted that he do nothing of the sort. I accepted his bed only when he agreed to sleep in the armchair in the room with one of his two blankets. When I awoke in the morning, my Galahad was leaving to meet a deputation of petitioners outside. No one was shocked when I emerged a short time later, and we all had breakfast together.

Another time, I was staying in Calcutta with a friend, whose shower-room window had no curtain. When coolies, who were working on a house level with the window, saw me under the shower, they immediately descended to the floor

* Mahabharata, Section LXXIV, Sambhava Parva, page 221, Adiparva Sections I–XI. Translated into English by P. C. Roy. Bharata Press, Calcutta, 1883.

below. I had no peeping Toms during the two weeks of my visit. Not even the novelty of a skin different from theirs could induce these simple people to take advantage of their strategic position. Had I been dressed, they would have stared with all the usual curiosity, but I was naked, and a woman's body is always respected. This is why an old-fashioned Indian woman, who will not strip to bathe even in the privacy of her own bathroom but always washes in a sari, thinks nothing of sleeping next to strange men in a train. She knows that being a woman she is safe; if she makes no overtures, the men will certainly make none.

To the outsider, most Indian women appear to be down-trodden. An old-fashioned wife walks a few feet behind her husband, she does not speak to him in public, she eats only after he has eaten, she never refers to him by name but addresses him by circumlocutions which vary with her education and the region. In parts of Bombay, *ikere, tikere* ('here, there') or *gharwalla* ('houseman') is used for 'my husband.' The educated wives of important men in Delhi still call their husbands 'he' in English.

No one should be deceived by this apparent inferiority. The position of the woman in the home is supreme. The man is a consort, to be humored and honored, but a consort all the same. The queen bee of the household need not be the wife; indeed, she is often not the wife. She may be the husband's mother or his eldest widowed sister. Only when the young wife of an old-fashioned home has aged into the eldest matron does she acquire that ultimate authority.

When my husband was administrator of a district before Independence, he complained that whenever he proposed a new idea to the men — such as a new school or digging a well — they would scratch their turbans, spit pan juice, shuffle on one foot, and say, 'First, we must go and ask the women if they agree.' With a sheepish smile, they would apologize, 'You know how it is.' And that *is* how it is.

Husbands on all levels of society bow to their wives. For

instance, a young prince, who had been at college with my husband, was sent to England for two years to work at India House. He went alone to London and found a house for his wife and got his children admitted to an English school. Then his wife changed her mind and decided not to go back to England. She did not even inform him. She instructed the travel agent to cancel her passage. She had not changed her mind to spite her husband; she had simply decided to send the children to school in the Indian hills, where she had taken a house. Her husband asked for a transfer back home.

There are many ways, big and small, in which an Indian wife controls her docile husband. The wife of a senior secretary in the Indian Government telephones her husband, wherever he may be dining, at 11 p.m. sharp to ask him to come home. As soon as the telephone rings, even if coffee is still to be served, he makes for the door with a smile and a wave. Neither he nor his friends think it odd. After all, his wife was invited, too, but she would rather stay home than spend an evening talking politics. In a way, she allows him more freedom than a Western wife who will not let her husband go out alone night after night.

Even a man as cosmopolitan and as sure of himself as Sardar Panikkar, one of India's leading diplomats, is a very pocket Caesar at home. The Imperator, make no mistake, is his wife, a small, sweet woman who smokes many cigarettes, speaks little English, and remains very much in the background. Panikkar told me that, when he was a Minister in Kashmir, she absolutely refused to receive the Maharaja of Kashmir, who had invited himself to dinner, because she would have to present him with a gift in token recognition of his suzerainty.

'In my homeland, Malabar, no woman is inferior to a man,' she stated. 'You are his subject, not I. When the Maharaja comes, I shall not receive him.'

Panikkar had had to excuse himself from the honor of the Maharaja's visit.

'My wife is capable of anything,' he said to me, shuddering

in recollection of other incidents. 'When I was Prime Minister of the State of Bikaner, she refused to greet the Maharaja because he keeps his wives in purdah, and she boycotted the court. And when I was Ambassador to Peking, she told Chou En-lai that she intended to visit Northern China with me. Chou had to have a landing strip and a road built especially for her, as she could not rough it the way a man could.'

The newcomer to India will find that appearances confirm his expectation that Indian women are subservient and down-trodden. For Mrs. Panikkar may rule her husband absolutely, but she would never presume to interrupt him in public, much less to contradict him.

Yet she and other Indian women are much freer today than women in patriarchical societies, where legally the man is everything and a wife's position is totally dependent on that of her husband.

Before modern times, the Hindu woman had no entity of her own. She was a mere attribute of her husband, much as lightning is an attribute of Jupiter. But she was an inseparable attribute; her husband could marry more than one woman but he could not divorce any of them. Legally, she had no rights. Her power rested entirely on respect for womanhood and on woman's universal gift for asserting herself, often by passive resistance.

Ever since Independence, the Indian Government has moved to make women the equal of men with a series of laws. First, a wife was made the equal of her husband with the imposition of monogamy and the legalizing of divorce. Then, for economic equality, she was given the right to be the guardian of her children and to manage their property until they come of age. This was a revolutionary step because a widow used to have no status in society and lived off the charity of her in-laws. Now she has, in addition, the right to an equal share in her father's house, even in his lifetime; she need no longer live with grudging in-laws and she receives a share of her husband's property. The wife has legally become

her husband's equal. Indeed, she is more than an equal, for
she gets a larger share than he does of their children's inheritance. Women have also been made the equals of their
brothers. They are to inherit an equal share in their father's
property, though in the Mitakshara system, where at birth
the sons get the right to a share of family property, they can
still get more than their sisters by taking their share before
their father dies.

The principal result of these laws will be that, as soon as
people realize their implications, future inheritance and not
present dowry will be the deciding factor in choosing a wife
for one's son. Moreover, the wife alone, as well as the couple,
will be independent for the first time. The dowry used to be
given only to the groom or, more often, to the groom's father;
the wife could call only her trousseau her own. Now she has
a share in the family land, and she need no longer stay with
her husband if he makes her life intolerable.

Legal changes, however, do not mean that society changes
its standards. Making divorce possible does not mean that
there will be more divorces immediately, for society still looks
upon it with virtuous horror. It does mean that genuine
hardship cases can now be set right. Already many people in
the cities are straightening out their lives through divorce.

Socially and politically, women today are the creation of
Mahatma Gandhi. It was he who insisted that women enter
ashrams and go on hunger strikes and *Satyagraha* marches.
He believed in the complete equality of men and women and,
therefore, he used women just as he did men to restore Indian
national self-respect and to get rid of the British. Under his
leadership, women picketed cloth shops and went to jail by
the thousands. Such women as Mme. Pandit and Rajkumari
Amrit Kaur are the result of his work. Gandhi was more of a
revolutionary than Marx ever aspired to be: Gandhi was
Revolution.

Today there are women ambassadors, governors, ministers.
There are women in Parliament and women social workers.

Everybody has heard of Mme. Pandit, but far more typical and important in the awakening of women are the experiences of women less well born.

Take the case of Durgabhai Deshmukh. She was married very young to a man she strongly disliked. After a very short time, she left him — something which had practically never happened before in the orthodox South. Since her parents would not have her back, she found a home in one of Gandhi's political camps. She was intelligent and determined, but uneducated. An elderly Gandhian leader noticed her and paid for her studies, because he felt that there ought to be some educated women in the Congress Movement. In time, young Durgabhai took her bar examination and became a competent lawyer. She organized women's activities. She was nominated to Parliament, where she was an excellent woman M.P.: not only did she know her facts backward and forward, but she worked very hard, bulldozing her way with unimpeachable logic. It was only natural that she should be chosen to represent women on the Planning Commission.

While on the Commission, she met Sir Chintaman Deshmukh, the Finance Minister, a widower whose wife had been English. They fell in love and, since Durgabhai had meanwhile become a widow, they were able to marry. It is hard to imagine two people more unlike — the plump little woman in her simple cotton saris, who had never worn jewelry (from the age of thirteen she had worn the dress of a widow) nor lived in Western style; and the refined Cambridge graduate, who had one of the most elegant houses in Delhi, collected precious orchids, and drank sherry of only a particular shade of amber. Their marriage has worked so well that Sir Chintaman Deshmukh, once one of India's best-dressed civil servants, now wears homespun, never drinks, and is so wrapped up in his wife that together they look more like cooing doves than the elderly people they are.

As women became educated, they began to look for jobs that would both please their parents and pay well. Women in jobs are more recent than their great number suggests. In 1938, when my husband came from England to work in the government service, the women secretaries in telephone exchanges and in private businesses were all Christians. If Hindu women worked at all, they went into the professions. They were doctors, teachers, and — if they were poor, widowed, and of high enough caste to be unable to remarry — very bad nurses who considered their fate worse than untouchability.

When the war broke out, there was an acute shortage of clerks in all government departments. My husband did not have enough people on his staff, so he hired a shy but determined Hindu girl, a college graduate, who came to his office looking for a job (she had a mother and two good-for-nothing brothers to support). Up to then, there had been no women in government offices, except for a few private secretaries. And the older generation was apprehensive about the evil effects of allowing Eve into the dusty garden of files. They soon discovered that they were wrong; in my husband's office work actually benefited, for she, the first woman assistant, was very able.

Now thousands of girls have taken government jobs to fill in time between school and marriage or to support a family. The result has been doubly important. In the first place, many women are now employed in all levels of the Government — some, like my friend Sumitra Gandhi, the Mahatma's grand-daughter, as senior government servants. In the second place, avenues of employment have opened outside the Government for Hindu girls from good families. Office jobs and factory jobs are no longer confined to Christians. Work for women has become so respectable that it is now no more extraordinary for an Indian woman to work than it is for her French or American sister.

The courage and enterprise of Indian girls is fantastic. For example, Sita was a Mysore Brahmin, a college graduate, strictly brought up, not allowed to go out with boys or to use rouge or powder. She was working on a birth-control survey, which meant living in a village and going about on foot to other villages. She had to persuade women to talk to her about sex — she who had had no experience with it herself and who had most certainly never been kissed by a man!

The number of working women increases every day, and their sphere of activity expands even faster. Women market-research investigators tramp the countryside, carrying their food and their bedding with them, sleeping on the floors of railway platforms, braving the sun, the heat, and the dust. Their day would kill an average Western woman, but they think nothing of it.

Why do they do it? Some of them, like Urmila, are in revolt against their fate. Married at eighteen by her parents to a wastrel whom she soon left, Urmila works to keep herself and her son. She does not weep over her hard luck. She does not reproach her parents for her marriage. She works. She knows that she can never get a divorce, even under the new laws, because her husband wants her back. So she works hard in the daytime and at night she studies to better her prospects.

A different case was the lovely demonstrator from Andhra, so breathtakingly beautiful that every man in the office looked guilty at the sound of her name, so modest and unassuming that all the women liked her. She was a manager, and she was waiting for her mother to arrange a marriage in keeping with her family status. She shuttled across India — by air, by bullock cart, or on foot — demonstrating the benefits of soap to head-hunting Nagas, to polyandrous hill women, to bearded Sikhs, to blue-black Dravidians, to timid Kashmiris. There was nothing to stop her as long as she was not married, for she had no private life, no boy friends, no television set — only her family, her books, and her work.

And what work Indian women do! I once went on a rural survey in the Deccan, southeast of Bombay in the heart of South India, with a market research team. This team greeted each new day cheerfully, no matter what the hardships. And the hardships are real indeed, as is evident from the conversation that started the second day.

'Fancy! These rats have eaten up my bag during the night!' said plump Mrs. Shah, looking at what was left of her food bag.

Miss Havaldar, her supervisor, laughed, 'So that's what the soft ball I felt against my arm was. A rat must have over-eaten and wanted a cosy mattress.'

Thinking no more about it, the team set off into the fields. Tiny Mrs. Dixit crossed mud pools and irrigation channels and tore her sari over thorn bushes; Mrs. Shah fell flat on her face across a stone; but they smiled and went on.

The villagers were too kindly and too simple-minded to ask what these women who looked like schoolteachers and acted like men were doing. They replied to page after page of questionnaires — confusedly, for their minds were not sharpened by use, and gratefully, for someone was taking notice of them.

'It is rewarding to see that some people come to us in our fields,' said an old farmer. As the sun set, his white-haired wife reverently kissed the investigators' feet four times and repeated four times 'Namaskar' ('by the setting sun I salute thee').

Off the field, back into the tumble-down taxi with the half-blind driver, the team bumped its way along. It raced the rising Tapti River, which had been blown up by a belated but powerful afterthought of the monsoon.

'If we don't get across before the water gets too high, we shall have to sleep on this side of the river in the car,' observed Miss Havaldar.

Mrs. Shah tried not to remember that she was in the heart of tiger and panther country. Fortunately, although the river flooded the car, it was not high enough to stop it. Torrents of water had turned fields into swamps. The next day, the investigators were as alert as ever as, standing ankle-deep in muck, they asked their questions. The car was stopped by a big tree that had been uprooted by the rains and was lying across the road. While the aged driver stood by shivering, the women pulled and pushed at the tree with local assistance.

'This is nothing,' said Miss Havaldar, smiling. 'Nothing at all compared with getting around that sub-inspector of police who would not let our taxi into Coorg because it was registered in Mysore.'

And at Nandurbar that night, Miss Havaldar's quiet competence frightened away the ghost that was supposed to haunt the traveler's bungalow.

Truly, Indian womanhood is on the march.

5

Marriage and the Family

MARRIAGE

India is a country of arranged marriages. Only aboriginals and the modern elite marry for love. Although arranged marriages may be the custom that most sharply differentiates India from the West, it is well to remember that it has been only a few generations since marriages in the West were arranged and that we, not India, are the historical exception. Even today marriages are arranged in some societies that pride themselves on being advanced.

When marriages are arranged in a close-knit, circumscribed society like India's, the family obtains a stranglehold over the individual. The result is to frustrate individual initiative. Pioneering becomes very difficult. As long as marriages are arranged, the only thing that matters is that the individual conform to the standards of his subcaste. It takes a true revolutionary to create the smallest precedent, for any break with tradition not only makes it difficult for him to marry but also may condemn his sisters, nieces, and aunts to spinsterhood; and in India for a woman to remain a spinster is such a sin against nature and the gods that people marry their crippled or mad daughters to trees rather then let them remain single.

An arranged marriage is a financial as well as a social transaction. A girl's dowry is as important as her looks or charm, and nearly as important as her connections. The financial burden of the dowry on the bride's family is crushing, and a considerable portion of India's indebtedness is due to the dowry system. The amount of the dowry is determined by the status of the prospective in-laws and the earning capacity of the groom; it is also based upon the dowry that the groom's father will need to secure a husband for his own daughter. Moreover, in rural India, everybody is perpetually trying to keep up with the Joneses, so that a disproportionate amount of money is wasted on mere show.

Fortunately, conditions are beginning to change. As girls become educated, their dowries are reduced, for husbands value more and more a woman who can be an intellectual companion as well as a wife. Also, the increased economic pressure of World War II resulted in a tendency to save on marriages. In Gujerat, for example, the groom's parents now borrow jewelry, and in the South, particularly among Tamils, many people hire bridal jewels. In Bengal, where most of the middle class has been getting steadily poorer over the last half a century, dowries are shrinking drastically. A senior administrator told me that he gave his daughter only half as many gold bangles as his wife had received from her father. In addition, his wife's bangles were solid gold, while his daughter's were hollow. He had spent five thousand dollars in contrast to the ten thousand his father-in-law had spent twenty-five years before; in real terms he had spent six times less than his father-in-law.

A series of questions comes to mind. Does the arranging of marriages petrify society? Does it influence for the worse or for the better the individual as an individual and the individual as a part of society? What is its impact on the relations between young people? And, finally, how does it affect the caste system?

The vitality of a society depends not on the arranging of marriages but on the values of that society. If 'to get on in the world' is the thing, if it is desirable and respectable to make money, a father will select a man with initiative as his son-in-law. Then society is dynamic. If, as in India, however, the ideal of society is not to get on but to abide by the established rules, initiative is not looked for and the arranging of marriages enforces society's stagnation. If being a good Hindu is considered admirable above all else, there is almost no impetus to change society.

Moreover, an Indian father cannot simply decide that he wants a son-in-law with a good degree and a secure government job. The son-in-law has to fulfill so many other conditions that the choice is limited indeed. Horoscopes must match. Subcaste and *gotra* (clan) must be right. And so on. Such conditions narrow considerably the field of choice and so retard the dynamic development of society.

There is another point to remember. In a society where the older generation decides what makes a good husband, change is delayed by one generation. If a young man wants to marry a college graduate, but his father believes that women without a degree are better suited to marriage, he will have to marry perhaps only a high-school graduate. When his turn comes to choose a wife for his son, however, he may find him the girl with the education he would have liked in his own wife. In such a situation, not only is social change retarded but individual development is often stunted.

The custom of arranging marriages makes relations between young people less competitive than they are in the West. As a rule, falling in love before marriage is out of the question. Western marriages are the culmination of love and sex. Indian marriages are the beginning of love. Competition comes before marriage in the West; in India, as we shall see, it follows after. In the West a girl knows that she is free to fall in love, and a man knows that he can choose his wife. Under these circumstances competition within each sex is inevitable. In India, however, a man or woman grows up with the certainty that he will be married, that marriage is as inevitable as the monsoon, that it is pre-ordained according to rigid rules of caste, subcaste, kinship, and horoscope. As a result, there is no need for competition. And when competition is absent, sex appeal is not only unnecessary, it is unattractive. This explains a strange paradox: Indian women are among the most beautiful in the world, yet, with the exception of aboriginals and a few socialites, they have little sex appeal. They seem to have a virginal beauty.

The effect of arranging marriages on the maintenance of caste is obvious. As long as marriages are arranged, caste will remain. The pattern of marriages varies in different parts of India, though, for the only common restriction is that marriage must be within the same caste. In Northern India, marriage must take place outside the clan on the male side, which means, in effect, outside the village. By means of this rule, marriage becomes a powerful instrument for social extension and for the dissemination of new ideas. To take a particular case, the one hundred and fifty families of one Punjab village were found to be connected by marriage with more than four hundred other villages over a radius of fifty miles.

In the South, on the other hand, villages are cut off from each other by marriage. Marriage between cousins and between certain families are customary, and a man may even marry his niece. As a result, the social radius of a Southern village often does not exceed ten miles. One of the effects of this social consolidation appears to be that women in the South are far more respected and independent than they are in the North. And they get on better with their mothers-in-law, to whom they are frequently related by blood as well as by marriage.

Marriage within the upper castes leads to the creation and maintenance of innumerable connections — as well as of some new feuds — all over India. From the moment a daughter is born, her family is on the lookout for a suitable groom. The groom may come from anywhere in India, as long as he belongs to the right caste. A Kashmir Brahmin from

Madras can marry a Kashmir Brahmin from Assam, a merchant from Bombay can marry a merchant from Calcutta, and a Rajput from Jaipur thinks nothing of marrying into Nepal, as long as he is marrying a Rajput. Thus India is made one by the cobweb of marriages.

In many ways, the arranging of marriages makes for a stable society. Even the size of dowries is largely governed by custom. But many Westerners have the same attitude as the Scotsman of my acquaintance who assumed that an arranged marriage between people of different educational levels or simply between people who did not choose each other must be terrible. He said with complete sincerity: 'Just think of it! You meet overnight in bed for the first time and there you are for life — the husband highly educated and Westernized, the wife semiliterate and stupid. Prostitution is less cruel.'

He was voicing a belief common among foreigners that the Indian intellectual married to an uneducated woman is torn between himself, his wife, and the modern world and is likely to go mad under the strain. This is not true. In India, as in the West, if no community of interests is shared by husband and wife, each goes his own way. Within the house the wife rules; outside, in the business world, she does not count. Yet they may live happily together, as did so many of our own grandparents who had nothing in common but their religion, their children, and their home. Moreover, if, as in India, the wife has been brought up in the belief that it is right for her to enjoy sex with her husband, the chances are good that sex will provide the couple with an island of satisfaction in the midst of their separate interests. An Indian girl is not likely to be frigid because she has not had to defend herself against overenterprising men. And if success in marriage is represented by sexual satisfaction and children, it is achieved in most Indian marriages.

Child marriage is an important aspect of arranged marriage. In the old days, marriages were often arranged at birth. In 1927, the Sarda Act made marriage below the age of fourteen a criminal offense. Now the age has been raised to fifteen for girls and eighteen for boys. But legislation is one thing; custom and common sense are another. The 1951 census shows that, in the villages, perhaps half the marriages had been in contravention of the Sarda Act. In the towns, of course, particularly among the educated, legislation is not necessary. Eleven years ago, when I told an Indian friend that I was married at twenty-six, he looked at me and whistled: 'So old! You *are* lucky to have found a husband! In my country, nobody would want you. They would say, "There must be something wrong with her that she hasn't been married already."'

But today no educated Indian girl gets married before her very late teens. Many are well over twenty and still single, and only old-fashioned mothers fret.

Whether older marriages are more likely to be happy is open to question. A good case can be made for child marriages when marriages are arranged, for the sooner people marry the better. The idea is to get the daughter away from her parents and into her new home. Some peasants still consider loving one's daughter a waste of time — 'watering the neighbor's tree.' Village mothers often breast-feed daughters for only half as long as they do sons and reserve the best food for the latter, because they know their daughters will eventually leave home, and their sons will care for them when they are old or widowed.

The trouble with child marriages was not so much that children were married — consummation did not take place until puberty anyway — but that widows of a high caste could not remarry. A girl might be left a widow at three years old, and she would be condemned to a dreary life. Upper-caste widows have no place in Indian society. They become poor relations, perpetual reminders of the wrath of God. Their presence at a wedding, a birth, or a festival is forbidden because it casts the evil eye. Their hair is shaven; they cannot wear a sari with a border, or jewels, or make-up.

Their food is rationed and regimented — no spices, only the most meager and basic diet — because sexual instincts must be suppressed. This fate worse than death was peacefully accepted by its victims. Widowhood was regarded as a necessary state in the improvement of the self. But, with more education and a new climate of opinion, widow remarriage is spreading to the top Brahmins, if not in the villages, at least in the towns. There are ever more advertisements in the newspapers asking for or offering widows as brides.

The Government has raised the age of marriage for two reasons: to reduce the increase in population and to emancipate women. Raising the age of marriage must reduce the birth rate. However, raising the age to fifteen will not appreciably reduce the birth rate, for very few of the girls who marry at twelve have children before they are sixteen. Yet, to raise the age of marriage to eighteen or twenty-one for girls, as has been suggested, might make for more complications in a society without domestic privacy and with all the usual rural pitfalls — from the haystack in the moonlight to the tall weeds by the pond.

The Government of India wants very much to break down caste by arranging intercaste marriages. The idea was Gandhi's. He married his son to the daughter of Mr. Rajagopalachari, ex-Governor-General of India and a leading South Indian politician, philosopher, and author. It was probably the first time that a girl from the topmost Brahmin subcaste had married a merchant. Recently the Government of Bihar started a scholarship fund as a premium for intercaste marriages; the greater the gap in caste, the greater the premium. However, this is a rash attempt at undermining caste and may bring harm to the cause. Intercaste marriages are a good solvent of caste only so long as they are successful and can be held up as shining examples. Therefore, unless they are love matches, intercaste marriages should be arranged with twice as much care as ordinary marriages. Outside of caste itself, as many factors as possible should be common — from diet to education, from the sort of respect due to one's elders to fortune. To make things easier for the lower-caste partner, both families must have a broad enough outlook to refrain from irritating each other about caste differences. Such a marriage will be as successful as a traditional one, and caste will have been weakened.

On the other hand, when an intercaste love marriage goes sour, as some marriages for love do anywhere, it confirms the old-fashioned in their views on the penalties of transgressing caste. Like all countries, India has its prophets of evil who delight in saying 'I told you so,' but in India their gloating carries further.

Love marriages are still very much the exception in India, but the younger generation is no longer docile. Perhaps the greatest victims of the transition are the children who are caught between Victorian decorum, reluctance to hurt their parents, and the desire to please themselves.

'When we return to India from studying in England or America, we say that we will marry only for love. Yet, I ask you, how many of our contemporaries have married for love? After much hope, frustration, and tension, we marry for horoscopes,' said a friend who had just bundled his younger brother off to British East Africa, where there is a large Indian population, to marry a girl neither of them had seen but who came from the same background. My friend added: 'How can it be otherwise when we have no real social freedom?'

That evening, six of us were celebrating the younger brother's venture, and we all had marriage very much on our minds. One of the boys said, 'Just imagine! A friend of father's was asked by his daughter to arrange a husband, and he refused saying the responsibility was too great.' We all laughed at the progressive father and his Victorian daughter.

'What am I to do?' asked another boy. 'I want to fall in love before I am engaged. And that is not possible. The moment I talk to a suitable girl three times, my parents want to enter into preliminaries with her parents. It kills everything.

I wish I had been born twenty years ago when life was so much simpler.'

I have had this conversation in some form or other with every young college graduate I know who has returned from studying abroad. I have also had it with every young woman who is no longer in her teens and is beginning to want to choose for herself; and with every mother, who complains that the young are unreasonable, that they take too long to make up their minds, that they are too demanding. My Indian friends think they are unique in their struggle with orthodoxy, although the same struggle goes on in orthodox Jewish and Catholic homes from time to time in the West.

Life is made the more difficult for them because many of the love marriages they know about have been less successful than the arranged ones. Of course the comparison is not fair since the numbers are so unequal, but this does not lessen their problem. As there are more love marriages, it becomes more difficult to bring about successful arranged ones, and young and old suffer. So far, however, the suffering is confined to a limited section of the population. Marrying for love is taking hold among the upper and middle classes; it has not touched the working class or the peasantry.

THE JOINT FAMILY

Now it is time to look at the bad side of Indian marriages. Competition, so notably lacking before marriage, comes after the wedding, when the couple settles down to live with the groom's family. His 'family' means not only his mother and father but his brothers and their wives and children, grandparents, and any unmarried sisters. It is a 'joint family,' where everyone shares with everyone else and no married couple lives a life of its own. The joint family is a key factor in Indian life.

It is the custom for married sons to remain under the paternal roof. A young bride has to fit into a new household, of which she is a junior and unimportant member. Mother-in-law is all-in-all. If the mother-in-law is bad, the chances for the bride's happiness are slim. Of course, such a problem is not confined to India: possibly nowhere in the world can two women, especially a daughter-in-law and a mother-in-law, run a house without quarreling. But in the West, when circumstances demand such propinquity, it is either temporary or the mother-in-law realizes that rather than exercising a right she is being done a favor. In India, the mother-in-law's rightful place is the home of her son. She expects to run his home until she dies.

Up to the time of his marriage, a son has grown up under the influence of his mother and sisters. In order to establish herself, a young bride must win him over to her side. The whole of her married life is at stake. If she does not want to play second fiddle to her mother-in-law and her elder sister-in-law, she must be backed by her husband. There may be fierce competition between wife and mother-in-law during the first few years. In the end, though, the wife usually wins, particularly if she bears sons.

The joint family is not a universal Indian institution. Much of India is too poor for the joint family to survive; for if there is nothing to share, there is no bond. Landless laborers who often move from place to place have no joint family. The peasant with a couple of acres soon finds that his son either moves into another hut or sets up his own kitchen in a corner of the compound; in the latter case, there are in fact two homesteads under one roof.

Nonetheless, the joint family has strong roots among Brahmins, merchants, and the richer peasants. Brahmins are bound to it by tradition or by status. Merchants find it a convenience for pooling brains and money and, more recently, for dividing taxes. Peasants with too many acres of land for one family have an interest in keeping their sons and their wives — perhaps even their own brothers and their wives — under one roof. The quarreling and the nagging of the women are more than made up for by the labor that is gained.

In the towns, particularly among professional people, the married couple is slowly becoming the unit as more girls are educated. At first they try to live with their mother-in-law, but soon they insist on moving into an apartment of their own. This is easier to do in towns, where apartments are overcrowded and where the husband has an independent job. Even orthodox parents no longer really expect their children to stay with them.

In the villages, also, certain factors are beginning to undermine the subordination of the marriage to the family among those classes of peasants who cling to the joint family. With rural underemployment and the growth of cities, men move away. The husband cannot yet take his wife and children with him because there is no place to live. As land shrinks and money enters the village, he becomes dimly conscious of the fact that his property belongs to his family in the personal Western sense, rather than in the collective Indian sense.

Times are changing in India. The standards of marriage and family life are developing toward the ways of the modernized West. But the movement is slow, for every step of the way there are restrictions of caste to be circumvented or overcome.

6

Sex and Family Planning

SEX

There is no Hindu Eve, no Hindu garden of Eden, no forbidden apple. Sex is not original sin; it is a gift of the Gods, to be enjoyed, like all things, in moderation.

Indians have the reputation with many Westerners of being over-sexed; this is quite undeserved. It is specially undeserved because, in this context, Westerners usually mean 'Hindus' when they say 'Indians.' Christians in India behave like Christians anywhere. Indian Moslems suffer from Purdah (the seclusion of women), but less so than those of the Middle East, and when Sikhs are wolfish, they are so in an almost G.I. way.

The Hindu attitude to sex varies somewhat from caste to caste, but in general, outside and inside marriage, it is characterized by moderation.

Outside marriage, except among the aboriginals, there is very little sexual activity; youthful love affairs are very much the exception and are much frowned upon. The average Hindu behaves much like the orthodox Jew of the Kinsey Report; he has hardly any extramarital experience. In the village there are no prostitutes, only the occasional obliging widow, who is still young enough, and who lives on her own, to whose hut the young man whose wife is not yet nubile repairs in the dead of night. There are prostitutes in the towns, but not as many as one would expect, considering the heavy preponderance of men in the cities. In Bombay, for example, there are six hundred women for every thousand men and yet prostitution does not force itself upon the passerby as it does in Piccadilly or Times Square. There is in Bombay, it is true, the ill-famed cage district where women are huddled three to five at a time in a cubicle caged off the street for their own protection. There sex can be had, without privacy, for five cents at a time, but compared with similar districts in Hamburg, Marseilles, or Casablanca, the cage district of Bombay is so miserable that it ceases to be obscene — sex in a cage for five cents becomes merely another excretory function.

There are the Devadasis and the dancing girls, but both are becoming more and more a thing of the past. The Devadasi system, by which parents consecrated their daughter to the deity and allowed her to become a temple prostitute, has become illegal since India signed the International Convention for the Suppression of Immoral Traffic in 1921. And, except in Bombay State, Devadasis are no longer to be found. Even in Bombay, they are illegal. The dancing girl has been hit by equality. Dancing girls were the prerogatives of the Princes and the big landlords; they danced, sang and loved; they have been the traditional guardians of Hindu music and dance; they had an honored place in the Palace. It was always a dancing girl who tied the sacred thread of marriage to the neck of her master's bride or daughter because, not being married herself, she could never become a widow, and therefore her action was considered auspicious. But now that landlords and Princes are abolished, dancing girls are becoming film stars and professional artists.

Indeed, if proof was required that Hindus are well behaved, one can look to the record of Hindu regiments during the war: they attracted no camp-followers and they did not fraternize.

In marriage, too, there is considerable restraint, for a series of reasons which range from the way Hindu homes are built to the belief in whole series of religious taboos. Hindus believe that too much sex is bad: they think that the seed of man contains his strength and his moral power, hence the virtue of abstinence. Hinduism, as practiced by the orthodox, is lavish in forbidden days, especially in the village, where one has not only to conform but where one has to be known to conform by one's kin, from whom it is practically impossible to get away. Sexual abstinence is expected during the eight months which surround the birth of a child, on all festival occasions (and there are many), on Tuesdays for some castes, on Mondays for others, on Fridays for still others, during whole lunar months at a time, on full-moon days, new-moon days, during menstruation and for some days after, on the day the husband has a shave and a haircut, on the day he has his ritual bath. The extreme is found in orthodox Tanjore, where Brahmins approach their wives on Fridays only.

The ideal of sexual abstinence is sometimes expressed in the way houses are built. In the South Punjab, a typical household resembles that of Ram Singh, a Delhi student who invited me to visit his father's prosperous home. The inner courtyard, in which most of the family activities go on, is lined with rooms — the kitchen, a number of storerooms, a cattle room, one room for the women, one for the men, and, in a corner there is a little room, scarcely the size of a big double-bed. Ram Singh explained that this was the nuptial room. The members of the family have to take turns reserving it. To reserve it too often is frowned upon. Ram Singh said that he could ask for it five times a month, at the most, and this only because he is newly married. 'We have no freedom to talk to our wives' he said bitterly.

The nuptial room is a practice of the better-off. Even in the cities it is often retained by people who live in modern apartments, partly because dormitories reduce the number of rooms required, partly because they do not have the urge to live as couples. The poorer people live in one room which houses everything — the family, the stores and the cattle.

With all this moderation why do Westerners get an exaggerated idea of Hindu promiscuity? There are many reasons, ranging from the existence of the tantric cults and erotic sculptures and literature to Devadasis, aphrodisiacs, and the high birthrate.

The Indian birthrate is in fact no higher than that of mid-Victorian England, or of 1890 Germany. A high birthrate is a reflection of lack of contraception, not of lechery. The tantric cults are a thing of the past, and they never were the belief of more than a very limited few. Their orgies were not intended to provide an excuse for sexual indulgence but to express the final unity of the female element with the creative impulse. Much as with bacchanals and medieval witchcraft, the act was symbolic rather than pornographic, and at its peak, in the tenth to twelfth centuries, tantrism was the faith of a minority of the people in a relatively small part of India.

Erotic sculptures are more difficult to explain than tantric practices, because they are so few and so divorced from the rest of Indian life. At Kajuraho, for example, the erotic sculptures which have earned the Temples their reputation for obscenity, at least in Western guide books, are no more than perhaps half a dozen per temple, and each temple has thousands of sculptures. These sculptures may be tantric but nobody knows. The archeologists have half a dozen explanations, none of them satisfactory. Similarly with the erotic literature. Everybody has heard of the Kamasutra, but few are those who have tried to read it. It is a sex manual so dull and technical that Kinsey, by comparison, reads like a thriller. The rest of ancient Hindu literature is a long sermon on the virtues of abstinence, self-control, and renunciation. Lust is always sordid, always punished by impotence, blindness, death, or some even more frightful calamity. Modern Indian literature is equally chaste. There is no Mickey Spillane, and the most daring love scenes would not make Jane Austen blush. The Devadasis were very similar in function to Baby-

Ionian priestesses, and, even at their height, they were never as numerous as the prostitutes of Western cities.

It is true that aphrodisiacs are more prominent in India than in the West. There are quite definite reasons for this. First, until a few years ago, the advertisement of aphrodisiacs was allowed. Secondly, so long as middle-aged widowers marry young girls, a custom which is fast disappearing now that the marriage of widows is spreading, it was often necessary for them to take stimulants to perform as husbands. Since Hindus rarely drink, they substituted an aphrodisiac for a quick couple of gins. A distinction must be made between the occasional use of aphrodisiacs by the poor and the addiction of some of the wealthy, however. There is in India a small group, consisting mainly of princes, landlords, and businessmen, who keep mistresses and swallow anything to keep themselves potent. It is their eagerness for aphrodisiacs which has made them famous and put a heavy premium on the rhinoceros, whose horn is credited with erotic properties. But even this minority of the wealthy does not use aphrodisiacs for seduction, as gin is used in other countries, but to satisfy their partner; according to Hinduism, sex plays as important a part in the satisfaction of woman as of man. Indeed, the Mahabaratha says that women enjoy sex 'eight times more' than men.

The keynote of the Hindu scriptures and Hindu philosophy's teaching on sex is moderation. It is a sin to approach one's wife 'outside her season.' Her 'season' in this context does not mean her menstrual period but her season of desire. Never must a man force himself on an unwilling partner. That is why, in certain parts of India, it is the duty of the priest, during the wedding ceremony, to instruct the groom in his duties as a lover, for it becomes one of his religious duties to satisfy his wife.

Hindus have, on the whole, a healthy attitude to sex; perhaps because so much of India is still rural, perhaps too because of this Hindu cult of moderation. In this society of moderation, in which there is no commandment to multiply, family planning meets with no such resistance as it has done in the West.

FAMILY PLANNING

Perhaps the greatest challenge to India's future is its population problem, which threatens the nation with slow strangulation.

As recently as 1930, the British Government measured India's prosperity by its increase in population. Even in 1947, when the British left, Indians thought that the recent decline in the standard of living was not due to an excess of population — as the British claimed — but to colonial exploitation. Many Indians reasoned that, now that they were free, the future was bright; the more people there were, the more food they could grow and the more consumer goods they could produce.

Yet, even before the 1951 census, Indians were beginning to question this theory and to realize that India's trouble was too many people for too little land. In the 1951 census, the population of India was 357 million; at the present rate of increase — 1.25 per cent a year — it will be around 800 million by the end of the century. According to Malthusian laws, this figure of 800 million will never be reached. But what about an increase of 200 million in, say, twenty years? This rate of increase — 1.25 per cent a year — is not excessive in itself. Even in Canada and the United States, the rate is higher; in Ceylon and in Mexico, it is 3 per cent. India's savings are, however, limited. Therefore, even a rate of increase of population of 1.25 per cent represents a great strain.

Now, moreover, the application of preventive medicine is causing the death rate to fall, and the rate of increase threatens to speed up disastrously. Thus, with the assistance of the World Health Organization and private organizations, the Government has introduced large-scale B.C.G. campaigns. It has brought dispensaries into the villages, introduced sulfa drugs and antibiotics, started vaccinations and cholera inoculations, and, most important, undertaken anti-malaria campaigns. Until recently, every year one million people died of malaria in India. Now the Government has begun widespread D.D.T. spraying campaigns; in some areas where malaria once raged, it is already negligible.

Indian villagers are only dimly aware of the population increase because children are as much a part of their life as the rains. Moreover, they consider pregnancy a blessing from the gods. Every woman wants children. Indeed, a barren daughter-in-law is a useless mouth to feed; she is a curse on her new home. To be sterile is terrible in any society, but in India, where women are still primarily wives and mothers, it is especially so. To understand what it means to an Indian woman not to have children, read Federico García Lorca's 'Yerma,' which admirably describes the torments of childlessness in a rural society where there is no escape from the neighbors, where everything is the will of God. Indian women, like Yerma, will go through endless mortifications for a son — pilgrimages, offerings, fasts, prayers, even co-habitation with holy men.

Perhaps more than the people of any other nation, Indians are extremely fond of children. Playing with his children is a villager's greatest joy. It does not occur to him that he might have too many: one more mouth to starve is not a matter for concern. And there is always something useful for a child to do, whether it is minding goats, tending a younger child, or gathering twigs.

But when villagers are made to think, they understand that too many children can be a drawback. The headmen of three villages in Mysore expressed this realization when they were asked what had been for them the three major events in the ten years before Independence, in 1947:

'First, the Health Unit came. Our women live. Our children grow. Then came the war: our crops sold well; we paid our debts. Then came peace: our crops sold cheap. Now the

Government won't help us to live and it won't let us die. Our houses are full of people. The children no longer die and the old go on living.'

I shall never forget a visit I made to a backward and old-fashioned village in the district of Sholapur in Bombay State. The elders in their rustic turbans talked to me of this and that. They complained about the drought, the expense of cloth, the rise in the cost of dowries, the poor quality of their cattle, the stagnation of leadership. I listened sympathetically and then asked, 'Why don't you have fewer children?' Shocked silence greeted my question. Only their innate respect for women, even women wearing trousers, prevented them from sniggering. Obviously, I had spoken as no woman should. One tough villager got up from under the tree, spat out a long red jet of pan juice, and began to make his way back to the village. The others were starting to follow when a very old man lifted his hand and said, 'There is something in what she says.'

His face was hewn in time, his beard was white, he obviously enjoyed the respect that comes with age. The others stopped to listen as the elder went on: 'When I was young, our village was prosperous. Each homestead had its cow and its ghee (clarified butter), and there were at least five acres for every house. Now we have no cows and no ghee, and there are fewer than two acres for every family.'

The men shuffled in silence and creased their weather-beaten brows in thought. 'This is so,' stated the elder, 'because we are too many.'

The men were now looking at me, all trace of resentment gone. 'Sister,' the old man added, 'tell us what we must do and we shall tell our wives.'

My first experience with the problem of birth control in India was in 1945 during a train trip. I traveled for thirty-six hours in a compartment with two married women: a Brahmin

nurse and the wife of a railway clerk who earned thirty dollars
a month. While we chatted, they told me how much they
wished to avoid having more children. I had some foam tablets with me and gave them to my companions. So widespread
is the need that in the same year, in a purely private way, I
was to give some of the same tablets to a senior official's wife,
to my groom's sister, to the cook's wife, to a Jat woman I met
by a village pond, to the wife of a rich merchant, until I had
none left to give.

Later, during a visit to a community project in Uttar Pradesh, I was taken to a very dirty village which was to be
sprayed with D.D.T. An old woman approached my official
guide and insisted on taking me to the house of a leading
Brahmin. It was a nice house with a heavy wooden door, bar-
ricaded with iron chains and wooden bolts. In the inner courtyard stood the Brahmin's wife — a pretty and frail-looking
woman, with a child in her arms. She told me a tale of woe:
her child was ailing; she had lost one already; she had had
many miscarriages. Neither her husband nor she wanted more
children because they were convinced that a curse was on
them. So they had decided to keep away from each other.

'It is so hard when we are young. You are wise. You are
foreign. You must know a better way. I love my husband,
and he loves me. But we cannot go on punishing these innocent children. And how long can we live like strangers under
the same roof? For two years my husband has not been
near me.'

Her distress was tragically acute for her to be so bold as to
ask me into her house, for Brahmin women in that part of
Uttar Pradesh live in strict seclusion. I had nothing to give
her, but I advised her to use the cotton wool and oil of the
village women, India's equivalent of the sponge and oil of a
French village matron. Before I told her this, I made her
promise solemnly that she would tell every other woman in
the village to do the same thing. Her face was shining with

gratitude as she promised. Yet I knew that this old trick was not the final answer for her — though it might do for other Indian women whose need is relative.

Before family planning can be established, three conditions must be fulfilled. First and foremost, people must want it. Second, they must know how to accomplish it, which involves more biological knowledge than many villagers have. Finally, they must have outside help, either from private organizations or from the State. An increasing number of Indians want to limit the size of their families, but unfortunately these are the people who least need family planning. (This is a universal problem, not peculiar to India: the poorer and less educated people are, the more children they are likely to have.) The ordinary villager is reluctant to face the problem. If you ask a villager how many children he wants, he looks astonished and says, 'Bhagwan Deta.' ('God gives.')

If you insist, 'If you were to ask God to grant your wish, how many would you want?' the answer is nearly always, 'Three boys and a daughter.' (If he already has that many or more, he will not wish for fewer than he has for fear of incurring God's wrath.) If you explain that God can grant his wish if he co-operates with Him, he blushes, looks down at his toes, smiles stupidly, and doubtless thinks you mad.

Most villagers want to have three boys and a girl. The need for boys is basic to Indian life. There must be a son to set fire to the funeral pyre of his parents and to perform their death anniversary rites. Also, if she has no son, a widow has nowhere to go. She cannot live with her married daughter, nor is it safe for her to live alone, because of robbers. The Indian mother who has no son is haunted by the problem: Where to go? What to do?

The Government of India knows it has to make people realize the advantages of smaller families. But this is not easy when people cannot read. The Bengal Government tried the poster approach. Half a poster showed the ruins of a dirty hut filled with ragged children and exhausted parents; the other half showed a neat cottage with a happy couple and two well-dressed children. The villagers' response to the good example was, 'Poor people, only two children.' The Government gave up posters.

Once villagers want to improve their lot by having fewer children, the next step is to teach them the facts of life. This may appear unnecessary in a rural society, where people see bulls mounting cows in the fields and, where with the lack of privacy at home, children sometimes see their parents. There is, however, a vast difference between knowing how intercourse takes place and realizing what produces a baby. I am certain that many people in India do not connect intercourse with procreation, or at least do not know the exact physiology of the connection. So long as such ignorance prevails, no real family-planning campaign can succeed. Once people know, they can adopt simple and cheap methods like douching or coitus interruptus, instead of resorting to abortion. A considerable number of women die at the hands of village abortionists. I was told that, in one area, after the third living son, a mother had as many as four abortions for every new child that lived.

The Indian villager is very old-fashioned and accepts sex education — which India needs even more than family planning — only from a medical adviser, a midwife, or a parent. Sex instruction cannot be provided by the village level worker of the Community Project or the Agricultural Extension Scheme. If he were to discuss the sexual life even of a cow — as distinct from running an artificial insemination center, which may be his job — he would antagonize so many people that he would cease to be effective. Sex education must, therefore, come from doctors, nurses, and health visitors attached either to Centers or to mobile vans.

The Government of India has included family planning in its Second Five-Year Plan. It will spend nearly ten million dollars on this program, and it is probably the only government in the world which officially sponsors such a program.

There has been very little progress so far, however, partly because no satisfactory technique of birth control has been developed and partly because of the difficulty of making people see the need for family planning as distinct from family limitation.

Various experiments in birth control are being conducted independently of one another in different parts of India. The first to receive wide publicity was undertaken in fourteen Mysore villages under the auspices of the Ministry of Health with the assistance of the World Health Organization. Known as the Ramanagaram Project, the experiment met with signal failure because it depended on the rhythm method of birth control. Dr. Abraham Stone, an American expert in family-planning, devised a necklace calendar of different-colored beads for the different periods of the menstrual cycle. Since every Indian woman adores necklaces, he thought he had won the battle. But he reckoned little with Indian taboos. For instance, the beads had to be pushed, one a day, in one direction only. The safety catch, which prevented them from slipping back, was made of copper soldered with tin. To some Indians, this conjunction of metals is inauspicious; to others, it is a fertility token. Then there is a taboo against women touching anything during their menstrual period. They had to be cajoled into washing their necklaces and using them again. Finally, more permanent snags developed. The women forgot to push the daily bead, sometimes for an entire fortnight; then, to catch up, they pushed any number of them. Many women refused to wear the necklaces because they did not want everyone to see them. And, children were fascinated by the shiny beads — green, black, red, yellow. But in a village hut there are no drawers and no place to keep things out of children's reach. The necklaces often ended up around the neck of the family deity, which the most mischievous child dares not touch.

In the end, the Ramanagaram Project did India one great service. It proved that the rhythm method of birth control, valuable though it is in some calendar-conscious societies, cannot succeed in village India.

In Bihar, an indigenous method of family planning is being tried by a woman doctor, who has trained batches of young village midwives in the use of cotton wool and oil packs. The midwives get a two months' course in general obstetrics and family-planning salesmanship before going back to their villages. If the cotton wool and oil fail, the midwives can bring hardship cases to the hospital for sterilization. This Bihar experiment seems the most sensible yet, because the method is cheap and simple; cotton and oil can be found everywhere.

In the towns, family planning follows Margaret Sanger's methods. Clinics are set up with doctors and trained nurses. They distribute — sometimes free, sometimes at cost — diaphragms and spermicidal jelly. There are more of these clinics every year. They provide an answer primarily for the middle and upper middle classes, though their effect is beginning to trickle down to the urban working class. But the Sanger method is far too complicated and too costly to be adopted by all of India.

In 1953 the Government made a survey of a backward part of Uttar Pradesh to see how people felt about family limitation. It was found that 60 per cent of the women and 55 per cent of the men were eager for it. Of the married women, 70 per cent stated that they would not wish to have more than three or four children in all, and that they would like to have them at intervals of three and a half years. A similar survey in Mysore in 1954 showed that in over 80 per cent of the cases where the wife was under forty — 712 couples out of 941 — both husband and wife were anxious to plan for a two-and-a-half-year interval between children.

The desire is usually to limit a family to the size it is at a particular time, rather than to plan ahead. For example, near Allahabad there is an old American mission hospital which charges money to keep itself going. A delivery costs six dollars. After they have had as many children as they want at home, women come from one hundred and fifty miles around to have their next baby in the hospital because, for an extra four dollars and a petition from husband and wife, the doctors will tie their tubes. Villagers who earn perhaps only fifty dollars in cash in one year are prepared to spend one fifth of that to stop having more children. Indeed, they are so many that the hospital has a permanent waiting list.

At the same time, vasectomy (the severing of the seminal duct) is becoming a popular way of limiting the family. A friend who ran a police training school first told me of it: 'After my men have had three children, I warn them that it is bad for them to have more than four. And once they have four, I do not ask them; I send them to be operated on. They don't mind. They know that I am their friend.' By the time of his death, this police officer had had forty of his men sterilized.

In the cities the number of men — from clerk to senior government servant, from teacher to Army officer — who get themselves sterilized after having had a few children is steadily rising. The dispensary doctor in one small Andhra town had performed as many as ten vasectomies in one year. But the most extraordinary of all the experiments along this line was conducted in Western India by the Demographic Section of the Gokhale Institute of Politics and Economics. They carried out a survey on village responses to family planning and limitation. This is what happened: A trained investigator, who had nursing and social hygiene experience, made a six-month house-to-house survey of one village. She talked of the rhythm method to women who had had at least one child during the past five years and who understood the connection between the sexual act and pregnancy. They were not interested in the rhythm method. Even when the investigator distributed free mechanical contraceptives, they showed no interest. But when the investigator privately explained the surgical method for men to a few desperate cases, the news spread like wildfire. Within a month, without any organized propaganda, twelve men applied for the operation. After much hesitation, the Institute sent a doctor to the village. In three months he performed forty-eight operations in that one village.

The lady in charge of the survey, Mrs. Dandekar, drew the following conclusions from this experiment. A division must be drawn between the attitude of the sophisticated and of the villagers. For the sophisticated, whether in India or elsewhere, sexual intercourse is one of many meeting grounds between husband and wife. They are sufficiently educated and well off to be willing and able to plan their families, using modern methods of birth control. But in rural India, as in rural areas in much of the rest of the world, poverty and a rather simple approach to life prevail. For lack of other ways of communication, the sexual act is often the main link between husband and wife. This does not mean that Indian villagers are haunted by sex. They are not. Extramarital sex is not frequent, and there is a considerable tradition of abstinence, which is due to fear of divine vengeance if one does not abstain from sex on those days when religion commands. By tradition, the Indian peasant is so restricted in the times he may have intercourse that he would rank low on any Kinsey list. At Ramanagaram, for example, a peasant never averaged more than twice a week even when the omens were favorable. To expect him to abstain on biological grounds in addition, is to ask him to be celibate. Finally, since the villager does not see the need for family planning until it is too late, he is likely to take the drastic step of vasectomy. Thus, the long-term answer for India's population problem is yet to be found.

PART THREE ✤ SOCIAL CHANGES

7

The Changing Social Structure

The foundation of India's social structure is the Hindus' belief in the four principles of Karma, Dharma, Varna, and Varnashrama Dharma (Action, Duty, Caste, and Caste Duty). Of these, only Karma and Dharma have a religious sanction. The other two are social developments which have been largely responsible for the stagnation of Hindu society.

To believe in Karma is to believe that what has been makes what will be, but also that nothing is inevitable at any point before it happens. Man is master of his actions but he cannot escape their consequences.

Dharma is a general code of conduct, like the Ten Commandments. At the same time it recognizes that no code of ethics has the answer to all the infinitely various situations of life. Each individual moral situation contains within itself, in different proportions, the elements that make up the code. For a Hindu there can be neither contradictions nor moral paradoxes. Perhaps the best way to explain this is to compare Dharma with the Christian point of view in the case of Graham Greene's *The Heart of the Matter*. To a Christian, the hero has sinned, even though he committed adultery not from desire but out of selfless love for another human being in need. According to Dharma, he did not sin because, in the particular circumstances of the novel, he did the right thing.

Thus, a Hindu judges the over-all situation, not each of its parts separately.

Varna and Varnashrama Dharma have made it possible for India to remain socially stable and contented. They are the basis of the cobweb of relationships — caste, subcaste, family, compound, street, and village — into which every Hindu is born and which leave nothing to chance, no room for an individual to fight against society or his group. His only way out, up or down, is through death, reincarnation, or a changed position for his group as a whole. There are no choices; everything is determined for him, from the way he knots his turban to the girl he marries, from the food he eats to the days on which he has intercourse with his wife. This discipline may be hard on the individualist, but it is most welcome to the mediocre, the conformist, the timid — indeed to the vast majority. From birth to death, the Indian villager need never venture outside the circle of his own kin. His kin may be annoying, but they will always have the understanding that comes from family ties. Therefore, he needs to make no adjustments, for to him, in a sense, there is no outside world.

In India, the fact that an individual cannot rise or fall beyond the range of his immediate society reduces initiative. For example, it would be utterly useless for a Sweeper to decide to be a Brahmin; he can never become one. Conversely, a Brahmin may behave very badly and let his caste down by becoming a thief, but he is still a Brahmin, even if a disgrace and an outcast. But, while the status of an individual cannot rise or fall except within well-defined margins, the entire group to which an individual belongs can rise or fall, if it is given leadership.

For example, I myself cannot become a Hindu because no Hindu would know what to do with me, where to place me, since I was not born in a Hindu caste. (There is a militant Hindu sect, the Arya Samaj, which does convert people, and some Hindu sects, like the Lingayats, convert other Hindus to their own particular sect.) But if I could get other Westerners living in India to join me, we could all collectively become Hindus. As a new caste or subcaste, and while maintaining our ways and beliefs, we could consider ourselves Hindu. Since we would marry only each other and eat only with each other, Hindus would readily accept us as Hindus.

Similarly, a caste can rise as a whole. This process began long ago with the admission into the Hindu fold of the aboriginals. It still happens today whenever a lower caste adopts higher caste rules, customs, and deities. However, since change must always be collective, it is bound to be slow, for everyone in the caste, even the grandmothers, has to be willing to make the change.

EQUALITY

Today caste is undergoing a series of revolutionary impacts, all of which interact in the traditional village to make for equality and a broadening of the villagers' horizon. To an outsider the village may seem petrified in the past, yet, to the villager himself, it has been ripped open by sweeping winds of change — change from within and change from without. The process of change in the stratified life of the village is so subtle, so all-pervasive that it is impossible to be sure of all its elements.

The most obvious expression of the new equality is the gradual breakdown of the restrictions against eating, drinking, and marrying anyone outside one's own caste or subcaste. Slowly, interdining and interdrinking are spreading from the towns into the villages, although intermarriage is still very rare and confined mostly to the upper classes. Any breakdown at all is both revolutionary in itself and a source of further change.

Migration, education, monetization, and land reforms have been the most powerful forces at work in undermining caste barriers of all kinds and in destroying many of the traditional village relationships which made for inequality.

MIGRATION

As land gets more expensive with the growing population, and since there is no new land left to divide, people leave the village to go to the towns. The emigrants are from two layers of village society: the lowest, who have nothing to lose, and the topmost, who have much to gain.

Hari, my second boy, is an example of an emigrant from the lowest layer. He comes from a small village in Surat district. His family is of the Rajbhot leatherworker subcaste of Harijans. To Hari, coming to town and working for a Western household is more of a jump in time than for Rip Van Winkle to have returned home after two hundred years instead of twenty. For example, he had never seen an electric bulb before he came to our modern gadget-ridden apartment. It is impossible to know how much he digests as distinct from how much he uncomprehendingly accepts, but there is no doubt that he is learning whether he knows it or not. He is a Harijan, but in our house Brahmins accept water from him and eat food he handles. This alone is a revolution that he is bound to bring back to his village when he returns to cultivate his field and patch his roof during the monsoon season. On the other hand, the extent to which he does not absorb the practices of a Western household is shown in the fact that he cleans his own room only when he is forced to do so. Yet Hari is personally very clean; it is simply that in his village, dusting is done by his wife. This attitude is not peculiar to Indian servants.

The emigration to the towns of men from the lowest strata — and their subsequent return with new ways of doing things — does not produce as great an impact on the village as might be expected. This is partly because their women remain in the village and continue to run their houses as they were taught by their mothers, and their husbands and sons dare not interfere. Hari brings back to the village stories about the wonders of the town, the idiosyncrasies of his employer, and a new concept of equality, but, unless he can mobilize his entire subcaste, he will not get very far if he demands that his caste neighbors treat him as an equal.

Only a few villagers work, like Hari, for Westerners or Westernized Indians. Many more go into textile mills, jute mills, or steel mills, or become messengers in government offices or rickshaw-pullers in hellholes like Calcutta. They have a different story to tell their village, but it is always a story of equality, a story which spells revolution in rural India. Theirs is a tale of squalor, but also a tale in which the influences of labor-union leaders, of Communist agitators, of Socialist candidates, and of their own caste fellows who have been educated and migrated to the town for good, combine to make them feel that they are just as good as the next man.

Furthermore, in the towns, people of all castes interdine everywhere with each other. They dine with Harijans in restaurants and roadside stands as a matter of course. In the village, however, the taboos against interdining have not diminished. Indeed, the occasions for interdining are few, even within members of the same caste. In most villages, there are no restaurants, no eating houses, and no social life as we know it in the West — such as a friend dropping in for a meal. Everyone eats in his own home except at weddings and festivals. That is why such interdining between castes as is beginning to occur happens mainly at weddings. The trend to interdining will continue. In the towns the sense of wrongdoing that was inherent in breaking caste by interdining is beginning to be dispelled. It is therefore a matter of time before returning villagers establish the practice of interdining in the village as well.

Village caste barriers are further broken down by the return of a prodigal son, always high caste, who has failed in the big city. His return damages his caste, for he is impoverished, his failure is known, and he may even have to take up an undignified occupation. A returned Brahmin who sold his land when he left the village may now have to run an eating house.

He cannot serve only Brahmins if he is to keep going, and by serving the rest of the village he lowers the prestige of the Brahmin community. In earlier days the Brahmins would have pensioned off such a black sheep, but it is hard to do so now that they are poorer and less organized.

While the return of the upper caste failure disgraces his community, the return of the lower caste success raises the status of his caste. For instance, the successful Harijan may buy and run a bus on retiring from a minor government job. And when my bearer retires to his land, his visiting son, who is a typist in a British firm, will bring him great prestige.

The exodus from the top stratum of villagers has had a far greater effect on village conditions than the exodus from the bottom. The exodus has provided India with its leaders, but the nation's gain has often been the village's loss; the village has been deprived of much of its own local leadership. It is as if all the boys of Gallup, New Mexico, who had been to college settled in Los Angeles, and the most educated person left in Gallup had never gone beyond the nearest small town with a high school.

Thus, the emigration from the top layer has meant stagnation for the village. But it has made for greater social elasticity within the village. As the upper classes turn toward the towns, they become less interested in preserving their power and the caste taboos in the village. The watchdogs of caste are weakened by modernization, and urbanization. Just as the Harijan is no longer willing to get up when a caste villager passes by, so the caste villager is beginning to lose interest in whether he gets up or not. 'What are we to do? Things are changing and will change,' grumbled a Rajput peasant, who said that five years before he would have beaten his tenant for such lack of respect. Indeed, a few years ago, a disrespectful Harijan might have been beaten to death.

The upper caste person who has moved into town soon finds that he can relax some of the more tedious caste taboos with impunity in the anonymity of the city. Eventually the village is affected by the same attitude, as the threat of caste displeasure, even of being excommunicated from one's caste, loses its edge. This leaves a lot of room for compromise with God in the village, as well as in the town. The advice given by an orthodox Brahmin woman to her son when he was going to study in England expresses the changing attitude toward caste taboos: 'When you are abroad, eat beef. The main thing is that you should come back educated and healthy. In any case, there will have to be a purification ceremony when you return, so why starve?'

What matters in such cases is not the fact but the appearance. I know an educated Brahmin widow who eats eggs, but only when she has trustworthy Western friends within her reach, for she cannot dispose of the shells herself. If a villager saw her dropping them in a field, she might be outcast. A Brahmin widow living on her own has to be very particular.

The main effect of the emigration of the top castes has thus been to make it easier for revolution to proceed smoothly in the village, without bloodshed, without vengeance.

EDUCATION

The steady spread of education exposes the village ever more to the winds of change. A schoolteacher who belongs to the educated unemployed class brings to the village ideas of communism and material discontent. Or one who belongs to the adjusted rural semi-educated class brings literacy and modern standards, news of plans and change. A schoolteacher who comes from a traditionally depressed caste is by his mere existence another step on the road to equality.

The profession of schoolteacher also offers a Harijan the step up the social ladder that the priesthood has always made available to the poor peasant in France. A duchess might not consider her confessor her social equal but, for the sake of his robe, she would invite him to an occasional meal; this would not mean, however, that she would consider his family acceptable. In the same way, the caste villager may treat the teacher as an equal in certain circumstances but will grant no special consideration to his Harijan family.

On a warm evening, the schoolmaster may sit under a mango tree, reading aloud from a newspaper. Those who want to listen have to cluster around him, for it is not easy to keep one's distance and also to hear. The Harijans may all stand on one side, as they are expected to do, but even in a semicircle the arcs must meet. Moreover, at school all the children sit together. Harijan children no longer have to stand outside on the porch, as sometimes happened under British rule. They may not always be allowed to sit next to caste children, but at least they sit under the same roof.

Although its role is underrated by almost everybody, education plays an immense part in disintegrating the old society. I once asked Mrs. Tarkeshwari Sinha, a Member of Parliament from Bihar, what she considered the greatest challenge to Hindu society.

'Make no mistake,' she said, 'there is nothing as challenging to our whole way of life, to our *Weltanschauung,* as education. Take myself. Before I could read and write, I really believed in all the superstitions that surround our religion. Once I was educated I began to ask myself: "Is *this* right, and what is the meaning of *that?*" And, of course, great though the ideology behind Hinduism is, not all its practices stand a critical look. So now, just to conform to the pressure of my elders who will die soon, I pay lip service to this puja and that. And I know that my children will do away with it all. What they will put in its place only God knows.'

One of the effects of education is to universalize religious practices, as in the case of Kala the washerman's daughter in the little town of Wai — a day's journey from Bombay — who insisted on performing at home a festival which is usually performed only by Brahmins but which she had seen at her school where all the teachers and most of the students are Brahmins. Kala invited her Brahmin friends to the festival and they came — with their parents. Never before had a washerman's house been thus honored in Wai.

In other ways, education puts new patterns into village life. Now, two high-school graduates of different castes have more in common — though on a different plane — than do two caste fellows. When every single vote counts, ambitious politicians will lose no time exploiting educational similarities.

MONETIZATION

Money has gone a long way to blowing change across India. With World War II came inflation, which put money into circulation around the countryside. Soon many villagers had enough money to pay off their debts and to liberate themselves to some extent from moneylenders, be they merchants or their own landlords. Thus, money destroyed many a traditional and semifeudal relationship, and now one villager in two is out of debt.

There was even more money around after the war. Food rationing was introduced on the tail of the historic Bengal Famine of 1943, in which three million people died of hunger. Rationing involved not only the distribution of cereals, but also their procurement from the growers. Since the small peasant produced at best enough grain for himself (in many cases he produced only a fraction of his requirements), cereals had to be levied from the bigger cultivators, who were paid in money for the grain requisitioned by the Government. Rationing brought about an economic revolution. Hitherto much village economy was based on barter. A landowner often paid his laborers with a share of the crop; he sold into market only what he required to pay his land revenue, to acquire more land, to lend money, and perhaps to buy jewels for his wife. He also had to pay something to the retinue of servants — common to the entire village — such as the barber, the washerman, the cobbler, and the blacksmith. Great prestige was attached to the ability to pay in kind rather than in cash. It is easy to see that this situation created a semifeudal relationship between the landlord and the people with whom he dealt. The war changed that. With rationing, the landlord received money for his goods so that he in turn had to pay out money for these traditional services. This sudden acquisition of money gave the villagers mobility, as money tends to do. It even made it possible to save, for money is easily kept while grain has to be eaten before the rats get it.

Thus, one administrative stroke dealt a severe blow to the higher castes and cut some of the traditional fetters that kept the lower castes in their places.

LAND REFORMS

The most important single factor in disrupting caste relations has been the sweeping land reforms. Since they began in the last century, they have steadily changed the relations between landlord and tenant. They are now finally changing the countryside as surely as if there were an agrarian revolution.

In the early nineteenth century, the landlord was the master of the land. He did not cultivate it himself but he had every power over his tenant who was by law, though often not in fact, a mere tenant at will and who was chucked out at mid-harvest if he refused to abide by his master's will. The rent he paid the landlord was exorbitant — usually one half of the crop — and he had to provide the seeds. The landlord paid no agricultural income tax but merely a nominal land revenue based on prices prevailing before World War I (in Bengal, it was based on the prices of 1800). He had the right to expect certain free services from his tenants, such as collecting wood, making cow-dung cakes, tending the garden, and providing food and labor for all the social occasions of his life, from births to funerals. He even sometimes exercised the *droit du seigneur*.

Land reforms have changed this inequitable situation and brought the tenant under the protection of the Government.

Eviction is no longer legal, unless the landlord wants to cultivate the land himself or unless the tenant has failed to pay his rent. The amount of rent has dropped sharply in the last few years; in the State of Bombay, for example, it is now only one sixth of the crop.

To insure equality the Government is doing more than protecting the tenant and fixing his rent. It is also putting a ceiling on the amount of land a man may hold — a ceiling that varies from place to place. (The land taken away from the landlord is paid for either by the Government or by the tenant according to a fixed scale.) Thus, the large landowners are losing power and more people are acquiring land.

Many people are sceptical about the effect of all this land reform legislation. They feel that it makes for more exploitation and poverty, because the landlord stops helping his tenant and may in addition evade the law and still get his old rent. Such difficulties always arise in times of transition, but on the whole, though, land reforms are effective — sometimes too effective. One day an old Mahratta gentleman came to my husband with a sad tale. He was bankrupt and wanted help in finding a job for his son. He had once been the owner of two hundred acres of good land which he let out to tenants. He himself lived in the district town. He had been a member of the municipal council and was the secretary of the local co-operative as well as an honorary magistrate, which made him an influential citizen. Now he is ruined. His land is in scattered plots of five acres each; by law he cannot take back more than what he can cultivate, and distance works against his holding more than twenty-five acres. He cannot evict his tenants to sell the land, and they do not see why they should buy it — it is much cheaper for them to pay one sixth of the crop and let him pay the land revenue.

The effect of land reforms on village relations is immense. Now that the tenant is protected by the Government, he need no longer crawl before his landlord. Now that the landlord knows that he has only a limited future in the countryside, he has to set about making a new life. He may use his compensation for the land he is losing either to improve the land he has left, or for new ventures, such as driving a truck, or perhaps for providing his son with a technical education and thus eventually with a government job.

SANSKRITIZATION

As society becomes fluid, the dispossessed landlord no longer wields authority over his tenant and he no longer either receives or expects to receive the respect of olden days. This state of affairs makes it possible for the tenants or the lower castes to move up the social scale — a process that is called 'Sanskritization.'

In practice, Sanskritization usually involves imitating one's betters. In Madhopur, for example, the leatherworkers' caste decided thirty years ago to become touchable. So it Sanskritized and began to imitate the Thakurs, a soldier-peasant caste. The leatherworkers gave up eating pig, marrying for love, sexual promiscuity, and leatherworking to become vegetarians and arrange expensive child marriages. They discarded their old caste name and called themselves 'Raidasis,' after a fifteenth-century saint. Like so many parvenus, the Raidasis are doubly strict in enforcing the gulf between themselves and their inferiors. To become respectable — to cross, so to speak, the railroad tracks — they gave up those characteristics that made them in our eyes more modern than the Thakurs whom they were set on imitating. Sanskritization is pulling them ahead by pushing them back. This they call 'a new wind blowing.'

WESTERNIZATION

Sanskritization is made easier when it coincides with Westernization. Thus, the Thakurs of Madhopur, whose customs the Raidasis copied, are also blown by a 'new wind' — the wind of Westernization — so that they no longer care about their status in the village. Thirty years ago — even ten years ago — they used to beat the Raidasis; today their ambition is not so much to keep others down as to urbanize and Westernize themselves. They no longer marry their daughters at five or six years of age but at fourteen or fifteen. They go to the towns and get government jobs.

It is well to remember, however, that, strong though the new winds may feel to those who are carried with them, they are merely a gentle breeze to others who are outside their path. Many people still cling to the traditional attitude, which was explained to me by London-educated Tara — so pretty, yet so obsolete. Tara, a beautiful Brahmin girl, said that when she meets a leper or a beggar she does not feel unduly disturbed by the contrast of her good fortune and his poverty.

'It is the will of God,' she remarked. 'After all, this beggar must be paying for old sins, and if I were to take a positive action to change his fate — let us say, take him home, feed him, get him cured, and settle him on land — I would not be doing my duty. I would be interfering with the ways of God and with the salvation of his soul. As for me, my fate is to have married outside my faith, a Harijan from Poland. Maybe I shall be reborn a Harijan or a cockroach for breaking caste, but I can do nothing about it, for I am only a tool in the hands of God. His ways are infinite and known only to Himself.'

But such complacency is no longer practical in today's India, for castes like the Raidasis are beginning to take their fate into their own hands.

CASTE COALESCENCE

The most significant change in the caste system is its progressive coalescence into three distinct parts. There are three broad divisions in the Hindu caste system — the twice born, which include the Brahmins, the soldiers, and the merchants; the Sudras, largely the main cultivating castes; and the Harijans, or untouchables. The aboriginals may be considered

Sudras although their assimilation as such is not everywhere complete. The relative proportions of these three main groups may be compared to a sandwich — two slices of bread and a filling. The bottom slice — the Harijans — is fairly constant in thickness. The top slice — the twice born — varies. The filling — the Sudras — is considerable everywhere.

India is divided into two regions — North and South — by the Vindhya Range. These mountains divide not only the waters of India but its caste system into two quite different patterns. Recalcitrant cloudbursts may change the course of water, and occasional caste exceptions may alter the caste pattern, but by and large the divison holds.

In the South, the Brahmins are less than 5 per cent of the population and usually only about 3 per cent; and there are hardly any other twice born people in this region. Others may claim that they are twice born but their claims are rarely accepted, and still more rarely well-founded.

The non-Brahmin upper castes are falling into their natural position at the top of the next layer, the thick layer of the dominant cultivating castes. They are also coalescing. In Maharashtra, for instance, most touchable cultivators have always been Mahrattas, but in the past in some areas they called themselves Patils or Khumbis, and did not marry with the true Mahrattas. More and more now they all call themselves Mahrattas and emphasize their unity rather than their diversity. Even goldsmiths will now sometimes call themselves Mahrattas. The establishment of adult suffrage has made unity a great necessity for them, for now they must agree upon a common candidate from their caste. With three quarters of a million people on the voting rolls in every Parliamentary constituency, it is the man who can appeal to the largest common denominator who usually gets elected.

The bottom layer, the Harijans, is split into a number of subcastes, of which only two are of any real importance. Division and poverty make it difficult for the Harijans in the South — they are usually laborers — to become equals. To become accepted citizens, they have to depend on the Constitution, on the Government's giving them waste land — and there is not much to give — and on the industrial growth of the country. Perhaps they will gradually coalesce into a broad group — the Harijans. Already many call themselves by this name, rather than by their individual group names. But the Harijans are too few, and the dominant castes are too solid, for the former to get more than a very minor share in power, even if they become petty peasants or industrial workers.

The Brahmin is almost the entire top layer of society in the South because he rejects all others. His numbers are small and his caste is divided into many subdivisions. It even has its untouchable subcaste — the eleventh-day Brahmins, whose function is to eat a free meal on the eleventh day after a death in the house where the person died. Until a Brahmin has eaten there, the house remains polluted. The eleventh-day Brahmin takes the pollution upon himself and, after the meal, he is supposed to spend fifteen days by the riverside to cleanse his body from the miasma of death. He seldom gets a chance, though, for death cannot wait fifteen days.

But coalescence is setting in even among the Brahmins. Educated Iyers, for instance, are beginning to marry Iyengars (Iyers are devotees of Siva; Iyengars, of Vishnu). This is a more revolutionary step than for a Montague to marry a Capulet. My secretary, an elderly Iyer from Madras, told me how the world is changing. 'One day Iyers will marry Iyengars as a matter of course!' he exclaimed, shaken at the thought of this great revolution.

The Brahmins in the South are not only divided; they are also heavily discriminated against. Under British rule, they monopolized learning and held most of the Government jobs. They were the landlords who did not cultivate the land and who often did not even live on it. On top of everything, they were the leading professional men and sometimes even the moneylenders. It was only natural that there be a reaction against them. For the last thirty years the Brahmin has been pushed out of his comfortable niche by land reforms and, through a prejudice against admission to college, from government service, and political office. Against his will, the Brahmin is being propelled into the towns and across the rest of India. Fortunately his long tradition of learning is standing him in good stead in India's expanding economy, where technicians, administrators, businessmen, specialized officers, and scientists are in demand. As he goes out into the world, he leaves his old ways, discarding ritual for the scientific approach. Because his numbers are small, the tempo of his modernization is so fast that he is providing once again — as Brahmins did in the great days of Shankaracharya and Ramanuja, India's greatest religious reformers — the intellectual impetus for India's national life. Discrimination is never pretty, but in this instance India as a whole benefits immediately. And when he is fully adjusted, the Southern Brahmin himself will benefit.

In the North, the caste pattern is quite different. The top layer of society is thick. There are many more Brahmins and an even greater number of people whose claims to be twice born have been accepted by the Brahmins. Perhaps as much of 30 per cent of the population can claim to wear the sacred thread. Northern Brahmins are less exclusive within their subcastes. There is no equivalent to the Iyer-Iyengar situation, although each Brahmin naturally considers himself better than any other type of Brahmin. The Brahmin in North India is often a cultivating peasant. He may sometimes have less land than the well-to-do Harijans and often much less than the Rajputs. He is a part of the countryside and does not keep himself segregated. He is neither discriminated against nor disliked; he gets along easily with the rest of the population. Therefore, he can stay comfortably in the small towns and the villages, and his contribution to progress is very limited. He is orthodox. Whatever culture he has is usually old-fashioned Sanskrit culture; he is more often a medieval type of scholar than a Ph.D. Politically, however, the Brahmin and his fellow twice born still provide the North with most of its leadership. The other castes are too backward socially and not well enough educated to have much of a say.

The middle castes are too split to be effective. In Uttar Pradesh, for example, the vegetable growers divide themselves into water-tight subcastes according to whether they grow or sell vegetables, whether they use canal or well irrigation, whether they grow pumpkins or not, whether their vegetables are grown in a village or near a town. Their entire attitude is in terms of caste. When a middle caste becomes important, its first action is to claim a second birth and to move up into the next caste. Thus, despite the fact that they are 50 per cent of the population, the middle castes remain ineffective.

One result of this condition is that it gives a greater opportunity to the bottom layer — the 20 per cent who are Harijans. In North India they do not divide themselves into many neutralizing factions, but mostly belong to one big group, sometimes numerically the biggest single group in an area.

India is moving toward a single society in which it is much more important to be an Indian than to be a Brahmin or a Harijan. In the North, a balance is being established with the Brahmins on top and the Harijans at the bottom. As both the twice born and the Harijans achieve this balance, they will begin to share political power and social position. Other factors will also be at work as people get used to this sharing. Orthodoxy will become less important; people will become more educated and economically more equal. By then the balance may be a mixture. Even the split middle castes of the North are beginning to unite; in time they, too, will be able to take their place in the new mixture.

In the South, the most important of the revolutions in the caste system is going on, not in the top or the bottom layer of society, but in the middle. The great central agricultural castes, who are coming into political power, must be the focus of unification in the region. They will absorb the rest. The process has already begun. But how will the Harijans and Brahmins fit in? The Harijans will be absorbed as the artisans have been. After all, they differ less and less from the great farmer castes in their way of life, education, and ambitions. For the Brahmins the only answer is to leave the Southern villages for the towns, where they can lead India to a new society in which caste does not matter. Southern Brahmins may be discriminated against to the verge of persecution but there is still no doubt that they are the top of society. If they accept those below them as equals, who will dare refuse equality? The future progress and unity of India rests on the shoulders of the Southern Brahmin perhaps more than on any other group in the country.

The process of caste coalescence is very complex and unfolds with infinite variations from place to place and from caste to caste. This much is certain: Underneath the maze of castes and subcastes, a new social structure is emerging, a structure based on new and streamlined caste boundaries. These boundaries are perhaps even more forbidding than the old ones, for they are going to be the last bastion of caste; once they start to crumble, the whole caste structure will topple with them.

8

The Leaders of Change

At each level in Indian society there are leaders. Whether aware of the changes occurring or totally ignorant of them, these leaders are taking the society of yesterday a few steps into the future. Owing to the waterproof tightness of caste, leadership has to be multiple. Thus, there are leaders in the caste, leaders in the subcaste, leaders in the village, leaders in the town, leaders within each political group.

Leadership for a caste must come from a member of that caste, and, to be effective, it must be followed by the caste as a whole. Naturally the leaders are the enterprising people who are more educated and therefore more ambitious. They know that if they are to rise in the world they must carry their caste fellows with them. It is perhaps remarkable that there should be any incentive at all within the caste to lead; yet there are leaders galore.

The main force for change in the village is the high-school graduate. When young Ram returns from school he can decipher the mysteries of the script and interpret rules and regulations, even for his respected elders. In the old days, Ram had to wait to grow up and for his elders to die before he could have a voice in the family. Now he is somebody at eighteen. As he reads, a fresh wind blows through the village — a wind rising from the printed word.

Ram may become a schoolteacher, and the schoolteacher

is a respected member of the village. Fifty years ago the schoolteacher was a member of the land-owning class. So great was his status and so unquestioned his position that he often served as arbiter for quarrels. Many a senior government servant today is the son of such a schoolteacher. Schools in those days were few. Today, when they are multiplying like mushrooms, it is no longer possible to recruit teachers from the rural aristocracy. Other classes, even Harijans, have been brought into the profession, and the schoolteacher's position has been weakened by the lowering of his class.

On the other hand his position has been strengthened by the great increase the villager attaches to secular knowledge.

An old Brahmin priest in a Nasik village grumbled to me one day, 'When I was young, I lived like a king. Villagers brought me the best of their rice. Today I hardly get a handful at festival times or when there is some family ceremony to perform. My sons have left me. One is working as a clerk; the other is an attendant at a gasoline pump. I have to depend on what little they send me to subsist.'

When I asked him why this had happened, he shook his head and said, 'It is our fault. We Brahmins have ceased to follow our caste duty. We mix, we no longer lead a pure life. The gods are angry with us.'

This religious decline is not universal. In some places, there has even been a religious renaissance, which means that more temples are built and more priests are needed. But, in general, the schoolteacher has taken over much of the role which the priest had in Old India and has increased his own traditional place of importance.

After the schoolteacher, leadership in the village is gradually being undertaken by the village level workers, whom the Community Projects and the Agricultural Extension Services are injecting into the very core of village life in the attempt to help the village to help itself. These village level workers are the most explosive of all the elements that are bringing about a revolution in the village. They mark the first time in Indian history that a government has systematically introduced into the villages a man with education beyond high school, a man who must become part of the village and who must not be considered an outsider or a representative of the Government.

If the village level worker does his job well, he will transform village India beyond recognition in a relatively short time by the sheer fact of his existence, by his example, and by the part he plays in the villagers' lives. This worker is educated for at least two years after he was graduated from high school, and in many cases he holds a college degree. He probably has lived in a fairly small town, if not a big one, yet he often grew up in a village. During his special training he has mixed with men from all castes and backgrounds.

Before the days of the Community Projects, educated men lived in the villages, but in a different way. The schoolmaster is usually educated up through high school only. He has had too much work, too little leisure, and not enough pay to keep himself up to date. In addition, in the last fifty years his status has declined to the point where his vocation has become a profession; the village accountant had great influence, but far too much power. The only other educated person who has had contact with the village is the touring government official. He has little influence on the places he visits, though, for he comes rarely. In fact, he does not even have much influence in the town which is the headquarters of his particular subdivision. (Equally, it never mattered how devoted the British Administrator and his wife were to improving village conditions; they never succeeded in touching more than the fringes of village life.) It may seem odd that in a town like Dhulia, with a population of eighty thousand, the permanent establishment of such officers as a civil surgeon, a district collector, an assistant collector, a police superintendent, a judge, and an executive engineer, together with their families, should make no difference to the way of life of the people. The reason is simple. These government servants live in a world of their own; they mix mostly with each other and not with those they govern. Theirs is a cosmopolitan life but it never throws out tentacles into the life surrounding them. They are above politics; indeed, they are forbidden to take part in politics. They are warned not to mix with the business classes, who might use friendship to ask for favors. They cannot be accepted by orthodox Hindus because of their unorthodox habits. And they cannot mix with the poor, because they have nothing in common with them. Moreover, they may come from another part of India and have no friends in the station, except for other officials and perhaps a doctor or a lawyer or two.

By contrast, the village level worker's primary job is to befriend the villager. The village level worker is not so far removed from the villager as to have nothing in common with him. Not only may he come from the same district, but he always speaks the same language, he will most likely worship the same godling, and his wife will often be like other village wives. Therefore, the way the village level worker lives, as well as what he teaches, is dynamite. When the person who sets a revolutionary example is different from the community, no villager will follow his lead for fear of losing status, for status is everything in the village. For instance, when the Prime Minister comes to a village and eats with Harijans, no one will follow his example for his status is *hors concours*.

But what can be achieved if the lead comes from within was shown in the District of Sholapur, southeast of Bombay, which was fortunate enough to have Captain Mohite for its collector. Captain Mohite belongs to one of the five great Mahratta lineages. He had no need to explain to the villagers exactly where he stood in the hierarchy of subcastes; they knew. What was good enough for Captain Mohite was good enough for all Mahrattas to follow. So when he grabbed a spade and dug a road for a whole day at the start of his 'Build your own road' drive, all the villagers followed suit. Brahmins and merchants, who are not permitted or accustomed to handling a spade, paid for stand-ins. When the Captain let it be known that his wife was studying in Poona, despite her large family, many a father must have thought that, after all, education for women is not sinful. And when the svelte, youthful Mrs. Mohite, with her fair complexion, her dark hair, and her lovely chiseled nose and tapering fingers, turned up during the summer holidays and actually helped dig trench latrines and compost pits, the laziest villager felt ashamed and the most finicky banished fastidiousness — the entire village worked. By the force of his example Captain Mohite completed an almost unbelievable number of projects in his eighteen months as Collector of Sholapur.*

After the village level worker comes the secretary of the village co-operative, an elementary type of accountant, whose advice is constantly taken. At present, there are not many co-operatives, but if the Government succeeds in its co-operative drive, almost every village will in due course belong to one and be able to draw on the services of its secretary.

Although politics in a party sense probably does not have a great influence on the fundamental changes occurring in India, it does play a significant part in the line of leadership. The local politician is a spade worker who lives in the village and runs the local party office. He has access to the bigger politicians; he writes letters to government servants on behalf of his constituency; he is the local echo of higher policies, which it is his job to explain to the villagers. There is not one local politician, but two or three, because not only does the party in power have a representative but the opposition also has representatives to keep the villagers informed about the failures of the Government and instructed in their rights. These politicians may be simple people, at most high-school graduates — quite often illiterate — but they interpret the

---

* A total of 411 schools were built of stone; 149 were repaired; 43 miles of road were laid; 126 miles were repaired; also, 195 temples were repaired; 17 gymnasiums were built, and 5 latrines, 13 trench latrines, 3 wells, and 6,490 compost pits were dug.

point of view of the Government to the village, as well as interpreting the village to the Government.

Visitors to India often ask me, 'What does the man in the village know about world affairs? He is illiterate, his horizon does not extend farther than the line of trees at the end of his fields.' That is only partially true. I visited a remote village in North Bihar, which is a particularly backward area, during the great famine of 1951. (Without an American loan of two million tons of wheat, this might have been worse than the Bengal Famine of 1943, in which perhaps three million people died of hunger.) At the time I was there, the United States Senate was debating whether to give India wheat. Mr. Nehru had told Parliament that he wanted no gifts. The villagers in North Bihar were reduced to eating roots, snails, and mango leaves. I asked those hungry faces, with their jutting bones and sagging skins, if they approved of Mr. Nehru's policy. They had been begging me for food, but at my question they stopped. With a recaptured dignity, they were galvanized into a single reaction by the mention of their leader. 'If Nehru says so, so it must be. He knows. He is educated. We are not.'

The local Congress Party secretary, barely able to read Hindi, said that he had explained to them that Nehru had their welfare at heart and knew best. He had heard him speak on the market town radio and he had taken his cue. 'He is a traveled man,' said the party secretary. 'He has been everywhere. He is a better Indian than any of us. He has given his all to the country; his fortune, his youth were spent in jail. He knows. I am an ignorant man. I have never left my district. So I must listen to Jawaharlal.'

The high-powered politician comes to the village only for the inauguration of a big project or the laying of a foundation stone. He also comes before elections to beg for that magic little piece of paper — the vote. When he comes to inaugurate a project, he makes speeches about India, but his speeches have little effect on the villagers. But when he comes looking for votes, he must behave like a servant instead of a boss if he expects to be re-elected.

In 1951, before the first election under adult suffrage, I saw a Union Minister transformed from an arrogant Brahmin into a humble man. I was driving with him along a dusty road when a small deputation of Harijans appeared. At once the Minister asked his driver to stop. It was blazing hot and there was no shade. Yet, he got out of the car and stood there in a cloud of dust for twenty minutes listening patiently to the deputation. When he got back into the sizzling car, he explained, 'They are voters.'

Such awareness of the necessity for equality, for building up the peasants' ego was in itself revolutionary. It may not happen often, but with each election it happens again. And as the voters become more conscious of their power, it will no longer be enough for a politician to come on election eve. Even on this trip with the Minister, it was apparent to me that the villagers had lost some of their former respect for the politician; they were expecting him to stop and listen.

We drove on to a railroad crossing, where the barrier was down. The Minister and I had to catch a train leaving in three hours from a railroad junction sixty miles away. We waited patiently for the guard to lift the barrier. Nothing happened. After half an hour I impatiently suggested that the Minister have the barrier raised. 'We must obey the law. There must be a rule,' he replied. We waited for one hour while the road and the fields swarmed with villagers who had come to see this incredible sight — a Minister being detained by a lazy guard. Finally, I got out of the car and asked the guard, who was obviously enjoying himself, when the train was due. 'What train?' he answered. 'The next train is due tomorrow morning.'

The politician does more than restore the peasants' ego. By telling them about the plans, the sacrifices, the success, and the failures of the party, he widens their horizon and helps build the India of tomorrow.

The civil servant and the Army officer also belong to the village. They do not live there, but they come as visitors. They do not even retire there, because the villages of India seem too backward to their new urban tastes. Yet their influence in the village is enormous. One of my friends, a senior civil servant, comes from a small village. One day I taxed him with selfishness for building the house for his retirement in one of West India's pleasanter cities. He was depriving his village of that enlightened leadership that brings progress in its wake, I remarked.

My friend replied at length: 'You think I am selfish. You are wrong. I have given the matter great thought. I am the pride of my village. They see me only for short times; they look up to me because I have knowledge and experience and power which is useful to them. If I say, "Do so-and-so," nobody, not even my great-uncle, will argue. They respect me because they do not really know me. If they saw how I live, what I eat, if they knew that I drink occasionally, that I give my daughters full liberty, that I have friends like you who stay in my house, they would begin to doubt me. Of course, the younger generation would back me up, but the older generation would be against me. Factions would develop, and I could not achieve half as much as if I retain my authority at a distance. When I retire, I shall devote my life to improving conditions in my village. I will come, give advice, go, and come again, but I will never live there. There is not yet room in my village for a man like me.'

Since the coming of the Industrial Revolution to India, the number of technicians has been constantly growing. There are two sorts of technician — the man with an advanced degree who holds a responsible position, and the man with a low-grade degree who does in India what is done in the West by a foreman or a skilled laborer. The first type of technician has an effect on his village similar to that of the civil servant or the Army officer. The second makes manual labor acceptable to his own caste. If a university graduate or a sergeant-major can oil a machine or clean a rifle, if he can cart a bag of cement or a crate of ammunition, he is helping to make manual labor respectable. And manual labor must become respectable if India is to become truly efficient and modern.

The factory worker often comes home at harvest. He is barely literate and unskilled, but in the big city he is the equal of anyone: he no longer keeps his distance from a caste superior; he is accustomed to being served food as everyone else is served. He has also become 'time-conscious.' If his day is not measured by the hands of a watch, it is measured at least by the blast of the factory siren. His rural cousin, on the other hand, has no idea of time. His day begins and ends with the course of the sun. Except for those few days when sowing or harvesting is geared to the threatening rain clouds, he can do tomorrow or the day after what he should have done yesterday.

In other ways the factory worker's life is broader than his rural cousin's. When the latter is ill, when he cuts himself or has a fever, he either ignores it or he puts a soiled rag on the cut, swallows some herbal concoction for the fever, or goes to the village quack. The factory worker goes to the dispensary when anything is wrong with him. Moreover, his rural cousin has an unbalanced and monotonous diet. He eats vegetables on certain festive occasions, not as a regular part of his diet. The factory worker eats a varied and balanced diet in the factory canteen.

The soldier brings back to the village the same kind of new habits and customs as the factory worker. In addition, he brings habits of discipline, and personal tidiness and cleanliness. And he is usually literate.

A domestic servant in urban Indian households is always a villager. Often he belongs to the same caste as his employer. For example, only a Brahmin may cook for a Brahmin. The domestic servant absorbs something of his employer's way of life, and he may even persuade his wife to try a new method in the kitchen.

Few are the women who bring back to the village the message of the town. The domestic servant, the factory worker, the soldier, even the lower-paid technician, rarely take their wives with them to town because of the shortage of housing accommodation. Until recently the politicians' wives were old-fashioned ladies who went their traditional way. The few women politicians wield considerable influence only when they stay in their constituencies. In general, this is the case with every modern-minded woman: she influences the village only when she lives in it. Her influence is practically felt when she comes to visit her parents. She does not try to teach them how to live, but in the course of her visit, she unpacks, as innocently as Pandora, a trunk full of revolutions.

In India women are the source of revolution, for it is women who bring up the men. It was Mahatma Gandhi's mother who sent her son to England to study after her husband's death, despite the opposition of the caste elders who excommunicated * the family. It was that pious, retiring little woman who changed the course of Indian history. Later, it was Kamala Nehru, a self-effacing, gentle woman in delicate health, who sided with her husband Jawaharlal Nehru when he staked everything against paternal authority. Encouraged by her moral support, he defied the formidable Motilal Nehru to join a little man called Mohandas Karamchand Gandhi.

The villagers are well aware of the power of women. Once I asked the elders of a Deccan village whom they would vote for. They all answered that they would vote for a woman if one was running. 'Are there no men among you,' I asked, 'that you must put your fate in the hands of women?' They shuffled and looked down at their toes uncomfortably until the eldest of the elders, a man of great dignity with gray beard and fiery eyes, thundered at me, 'And you yourself a woman! You ask us this. If we vote for a woman, it is because we want progress. If we vote for a man, he will not influence us much.

* Caste excommunication, like excommunication from the Roman Catholic Church, is the last sanction against offenders.

But if we vote for a woman, she will not only influence us a little, she will influence her husband and her children. It is through women that one educates people not through men. If I were the Government, I would not bother to send boys to school, only girls. That would shame the boys into learning and the mothers would be there to teach them.'

The elder had put his finger on an important factor holding society back — ignorant mothers and conservative wives. I once knew a man, educated abroad from childhood, who, at the instance of his wife and her mother, resorted to exorcism rather than go to a doctor when their only child was dying of blood poisoning. Penicillin had not yet been discovered, but sulfa drugs would have saved the child's life.

It is easier for women in India to assert their will on their men than for women in the West. Paradoxically, the source for their unquestioned influence is their complete subservience. In India, women swathe men in a motherliness that is all-embracing. Whether it is little sister carrying baby brother so that he does not cry, or the growing daughter who submits to an unhappy marriage rather than upset her father, or the educated woman who never disagrees with her husband in public, even if he makes a fool of himself — Indian women are always loving and maternal to their men. Therefore, to a man it would seem selfish in the extreme not to give way to his wife or mother over the running of daily life.

Thus, the Indian village is not an oasis in the desert. It is intimately connected with the town. There is a constant flow from town to village. Every Indian comes from a village. At some point in his life every Indian goes back to his village — for the death of his grandmother, for the wedding of his cousin, to look after the ancestral hut, or to find a wife. Every person who returns to the village — the politician, the civil servant, the technician, the factory worker, the domestic servant, and the women — brings with him the lessons of change.

India is not all villages. Perhaps 20 per cent of the people live in towns, and the towns are growing all the time in size and number. They have their share of leaders, too.

The Administrators who live in a town bring a modern outlook to their way of life. Some of them have even done away with dowries and, thanks to their powerful position, they get away with it. Their example is slowly being followed. Even if they are still very old-fashioned, they will send their daughters to college and increasingly they will send their sons into business — a thing that few fathers outside of the merchant castes would have done in the old days.

The businessman is hacking another step in the ladder of leadership. In the past nobody who was anybody would have chosen business as a way of earning a living. Today business is as attractive as the Government. Even the Brahmins have taken to it easily and readily. Formerly, many Indian businessmen were half-baked third cousins of the robber barons, untrained except in tax evasion. Concerned solely with quick and easy profits, they spent much of their time keeping treble books — one for the income tax, one for their partners, one for themselves. But now there is an ever-growing vanguard of businessmen who are managers. They bring to their new position of responsibility a strong sense of patriotism. As managers grow in number and stature, their impact upon Indian thought will be tremendous. They are the brothers, the first cousins, or the second nephews of the civil servants and the politicians, through whom they can exercise great influence on the Government's policies and on India's future.

But the most dynamic element of Indian towns is the clerk. He has the key role in effecting change. He is a man with a degree — usually a Bachelor of Arts — who is in daily contact with methods of thought that are not his mother's. His livelihood depends on using at all times the skill of the West. He is moulded in precision, he comes to the office on time, and he does a given job every day of his life in a given way.

There are two types of clerk, each equally important. There is the old type, the middle-aged Brahmin who lives in two worlds. He carefully packs the modern world of his office into his briefcase when he goes home at night. Upon entering his house, he folds away trousers and tie and dons his dhoti, thus re-entering unchanged the world of his forefathers — a cozy, orderly world where Brahmins are orthodox and respected, where it is expected that a clerk's son will be a clerk in his turn. 'When I put on my shirt, I take off my caste, and when I take off my shirt, I put on my caste,' explained one clerk to a sociologist.

For such a man there is a rigid balance and organization in his daily life. For instance, during the visit of the Russian leaders to India in the late autumn of 1955, one clerk said to me, 'I am grateful to Marshal Bulganin and Mr. Khrushchev. I went to the waterfront to watch the procession. I could not catch a glimpse because of the crowd, but for the first time in my life I saw the waterfront, and it is simply beautiful.'

He has lived in a Bombay suburb for twenty years and yet he had never bothered to go near the sea. He spends his spare time at South Indian musical recitals and discussing the customs of the South with his South Indian friends.

There is, however, another type of clerk, whose worlds are integrating; the old Eastern circle is overlapping the modern circle, and the result is a blurred zone in between. If the old circle wins, this clerk may be a trifle progressive, but he will be disillusioned and reconciled to the slow swallowing of his ego by the octopus of tradition. If the modern circle proves stronger, he will transform India.

Here is what happens in practice. Young Gangadharan — my husband's secretary — a lanky and handsome youth, is twenty-three years old. From the age of ten, he showed promise at the Mission School. His father, a semi-literate Brahmin from the coast of Malabar, lived in poverty, with only the produce from two and a half coconut trees and a salary of five dollars a month. His illiterate mother worked hard. There were four daughters and three sons to feed and clothe on five dollars a month and two and a half coconut trees. From an early age, Gangadharan was taught the value of money and the value of education as a means to getting more money. But in education he found a reward that outweighed mere payment in cash: he discovered in it the key to a wider horizon. He learned the satisfaction of knowledge for its own sake. He decided to go on learning all the time. After graduation from high school he went to Bombay to take a job as a junior stenographer at twenty-five dollars a month. Instead of spending that money on the movies, South Indian music, or cups of tea, he spent it on studying. He got promoted to a secretary at fifty dollars a month. But this was not enough; for he began taking morning and evening courses toward an A.B. both to improve his prospects and for the fun of it. Gangadharan's mind is quicksilver; his poise is perfect; the world is his oyster. His interest stops at nothing. He wants to get an M.A. in economics, French, and accounting.

Now he earns a hundred dollars a month. He spends only twenty-five of that on himself. He saves the rest to send home and to lay some money by for his sister's dowries. The eldest sister is semi-literate, but the others are being educated because Gangadharan's parents found it very difficult to get a husband for their semi-literate daughter. Five years ago, their neighbors thought it was a heinous sin to send a girl to school after she was thirteen; now they do not mind sending their girls even after they are sixteen. Gangadharan cannot consider marrying before his elder brother, for back in Malabar people would say, 'There must be something wrong with him if his younger brother got married first.' If the villagers think something is wrong with the elder brother, not only will he find it hard to make a suitable match but he will receive a reduced dowry as well. So Gangadharan cannot afford to fall in love at the moment; as a result, he does not mix with girls. He realizes the injustice of the system, but he feels a duty to his family. If someone saw him going to the movies with a girl in Bombay, his village in distant Malabar (one of the most orthodox villages in India) would eventually hear of it and would impute immoral motives to him and to his parents. Then nobody would marry his sisters. His orthodox society makes no distinction between the behavior of the individual and that of his kin.

If after his brother gets married he falls in love, Gangadharan may perhaps decide that his life is his own. If he does and marries for love, India will be rocked to its roots. For it is the young men like Gangadharan who set the pace. It is not nearly so effective for Nehru's daughter to marry a Parsi as it would be for Gangadharan to marry for love, even within his own subcaste. India is full of young people who are waiting for a lead from their equals; change is so much easier when it is collective and does not involve pioneering. For example, a girl I know married her first cousin against the rules of her particular subcaste. She was the first ever to take this jump. Within two years, there had been at least three other cousin marriages in her community.

After the clerks, the most revolutionary group are the urbanized Indian women. There has already been mention of the tremendous change in women's position in society. That is only partly the story, however, for these modern-minded women are having a major role in revolutionizing India.

Imagine an orthodox, strictly vegetarian wife who, for her husband's sake, cooks meat when she entertains strangers! She may grumble at the first stranger, but in time she grows to be fond of her guests. And she may even become so Westernized as to keep a pet dog in the house, a most radical step. Traditionally, the dog, like the pig, is considered unclean because he is a natural scavenger. In the village dogs are used to chase away outsiders. Only the lowest people touch dogs, let alone have them in the house.

Change is not limited, however, to keeping dogs. Daughters are getting a modern education and going into professions. They become college teachers or doctors. I have a friend who is an agricultural expert. After getting an A.B. in India, Uma went to England to take a course in agricultural engineering. She was the first woman ever to take that course and she stood first in her class. In India, howerer, she is finding it difficult to make a place for herself. She is not only an agricultural engineer but also a beautiful and frail-looking girl. It would not be safe for her to live alone on a farm. She does not want to teach in a Government agricultural college because she wants to be independent. She does not want to marry unless love comes her way. What is she to do? At present, she is raising poultry in her father's backyard. This is completely revolutionary for a girl of her caste, for, except in the South, hen-raising is traditionally a Harijan or aboriginal occupation. She raises hens in a scientific manner; and she does the work herself. She even delivers eggs. Her entire family has become hen-minded and gives her a hand. Her mother, who has never eaten an egg, nevertheless mixes chicken feed.

She is unique, but her four sisters are typical of the new upper class. The eldest, who was married at seventeen, is working as an account executive in an advertising agency in Bombay; she does not need the money but, with her son at school, she likes the independence of her job. Another sister teaches in a girls' college; no marriage will be arranged for her. The two youngest want to become a secretary and a doctor. One decade ago — indeed, when the eldest daughter was married — girls were married after school or college. They did nothing as undignified as earn their living. Married women certainly did not go out to work unless there was some very good but sad reason for their doing so.

Another girl, the daughter of one of India's richest businessmen, broke with all tradition. Normally, she would have married between seventeen and twenty-three. Instead, at seventeen Malti came by herself to Bombay to study. At first, her father cut her off, so she roughed it in a little room with help on the sly from her mother, and she took a course in social science. When her father realized her sincerity, he gave her an allowance. After graduation, she took a job as

Labour Welfare Officer. Now at thirty, she is still working and unmarried because, as she puts it, 'I am wedded to my job.' Society is reconciled to her going her own way. She lives alone in a large apartment and nobody gossips about her. She has set a precedent for the exceptional few who want to live as she does.

More and more Indian girls work and continue to work after marriage, even after they have children. This is easier in India than in the West, for there is no shortage of domestic servants or of relatives to look after children. Women are entering public service. There are several women now in the Administrative Service running districts and subdivisions, and a few more regular appointments in the Foreign Service. And there is an ever-growing number of women who work in offices. As women become educated and, with education, independent, they are becoming a formidable cog in the wheel of change rolling across India.

9

East Wind — West Wind

Winds of change blow from the towns to the villages and from the villages to the towns. Information is exchanged by villagers and town dwellers in age-old ways and in modern ones. Little by little, the tight world of Indian society is breaking down.

Besides the cobweb of marriages, which has linked many villages and some states, there are the traditional opportunities for villagers to meet and exchange ideas. In the larger villages, there is the weekly market, where villagers go to chat as well as to trade. There are the big fairs, the melas. Some are month-long cattle fairs. People and cattle come from many miles to these annual fairs. I have seen herds of cattle trekking over the roads for hundreds of miles on their way to a huge annual cattle fair. Half a million head of cattle may gather at such a fair: the best studs from the West Coast, the best cows from Hariana, the sad Modigliani-faced Mysore cows with their horns pointed backwards, the little Dhani cows with their black and white spots, like overgrown Dalmatians, the shiny hippopotamus-like water buffaloes with their pale blue eyes and white star, the impertinent-looking Bengali bull with his fat hump dangling on the side and his fish eyes curving upward — the best cattle and the worst. The civil authorities supply tents, drinking taps, and troughs. Traders bring fodder, bangles, tinsel, and sweetmeats. Snake-charmers, puppeteers, cloth merchants, beggars, lepers, fakirs, and prostitutes, as well as Indian villagers gather for these events.

Then, there is the holy pilgrimage. Hindu pilgrims cross the length and breadth of the country by train, on foot, in bullock carts. They pass through cities, they stay in camps, they meet people from the four corners of India. In 1953, on the peak day of the Kumbh-Mela at Allahabad, the great mela of the century, at least five million pilgrims bathed together in the holy waters of the Ganges. During this mela, which lasted three months, sanitary habits were enforced upon villagers: they had to use latrines, instead of going into the fields, as they were accustomed to do; they had to be inoculated against cholera and smallpox.

The process of change would be quite slow, however, if it depended on traditional means of spreading information. Now modern methods and technology are bringing to the villages the revolutionary messages of modernization and equality.

COMMUNICATIONS

Communications are opening up villages, as the Government's road program slowly spreads its network over the country. With roads come the bus. To understand how revolutionary the bus is, it is necessary to look back to the days when the only way to get to market was on foot or by slow and uncomfortable bullock cart. Now the time saved in riding the bus must be used to earn money for the fare. Thus, a major change not only in means of communication but in the concept of time has been introduced into village life — time has become money in the real sense. The bus also breaks down caste barriers. Both the Harijan and the Brahmin can ride the bus for the price of the fare. It is difficult indeed to maintain ritual distances in a crowded Indian bus in which hens, leather goods, and men are all squeezed together. If the Brahmin protests that the hens pollute him, the bus driver will point out that the Brahmin need not travel in the bus. He knows that throwing out the Harijan and his hens would not only be bad business, but might even cost him his license if the discrimination came to the notice of the Government.

ELECTRICITY

Big multipurpose dams are gradually bringing electricity to many a backward area. Electricity! Imagine a village that has never had electricity! What a revolution in the phenomenon which hums along the wires, shines in the little bulb that keeps the night at bay, and brings water to the earth's surface as if by magic, thus relieving bullocks and giving women free time! Electricity is the spirit of the loom, the grinder of the grain, the bringer of news, the enemy of fear and darkness. Young people avidly count the days remaining before their village gets the new goddess of light and power. Some of the old moan their fear, for they have seen its danger.

'Let electricity come and we will put up small-scale industries. We will make money and become like the people in town,' said the young men of a Deccan village. 'We have slaved at the loom long enough; with electricity each house can become a small factory.'

'Let electricity come,' said their elders, 'and we shall lose our old contentment, we shall get poorer and become worse men. With electricity people will be able to see inside their neighbors' houses and they will want as many things as the neighbors have — and more. They will no longer be happy. Today we go to bed with the sun; at the most, we sit around the fire and talk of God and the caste. Who knows what will happen when the sun sets no more in our houses?'

NEWSPAPERS

With the spread of literacy, there has been inevitably a spread of information. At present only 20 per cent of India's population can read, but it is estimated that by the end of 1960, 60 per cent of the children will be at school. Of the more than three hundred newspapers in India, some reach the village perhaps once a fortnight when someone brings one from the town. The schoolteacher or a visitor reads the news aloud to an appreciative audience. They make a social gathering of it, squatting under the shade of a tree, smoking their hookas or bidis (country cigarettes). Much in the newspapers is too difficult — or, rather, too remote — for villagers to understand, but they nonetheless like to feel that everything, every printed word, has been read to them. For days afterward, the elders discuss an item about a temple or a new fertilizer, until another newspaper comes with fresher news.

The standards of the Indian press are very high; editors are well informed and they try to be fair. There is no sensationalism; even the small Indian-language newspapers are similar to the *Manchester Guardian* or the *Christian Science Monitor* in tone. There is no Indian equivalent to the *Daily Mirror* or the *Chicago Tribune*, and there is no *News of the World.** Crime is never exploited; it is usually confined to the drabbest of items either from police records or from court verdicts. There is no tradition of following a case from day to day. Sex is rarely mentioned in the Indian press. The eyelid lowered on sex crimes is so Victorian that the reader is left guessing, even in the rare cases in which a woman has been attacked. The only time sex offenses are emphasized — always in an abstract form — is when rape is used as a political weapon by one community against another, as happened in the riots preceding partition.

Foreign political news is fairly and fully covered in the Indian press. There is no conscious attempt to distort, so that any distortions stem not from evil motives but from ignorance of the local conditions of foreign countries. Some of the adverse criticism of the United States is a result of this ignorance. (The same is often true of the treatment of India in the American press.) Indian politics is always extensively

* The *News of the World*, which with seven million copies has England's largest circulation, specializes in crime and sex.

reported and usually with astonishing accuracy. With a few exceptions, editorials are liberal, neither revolutionary nor reactionary.

The Indian press lacks a tradition of reporting what lies behind the news and the speeches, though. Above all, it fails to report what goes on in the villages. These shortcomings are partly financial, for Indian newspapers are always short of money. Very few of them have more than a couple of good reporters in the three or four major cities. Gathering the rest of the news is left to struggling local correspondents, like the Jullundur representative of all the major Indian- and English-language dailies, who may earn as much as forty dollars in a month when something big happens — such as a flood, a border incident (Jullundur is near the Pakistani border), or the visit of a Minister. Even in the large cities, the techniques of reporting have yet to be developed. Reporting is a new technique, even in the West, and in India too much of the day-to-day newspaper work is done by reporters whose constant struggle to make ends meet on twenty dollars a month — they may be elderly and have children to educate — leaves them without time to develop the intellectual curiosity that makes for individual reporting. Too often, reporters from different newspapers pool one story or stick to the official handout without comments. They dealt thus with a convention of African students in 1956. These students had grievances against their host country as well as plans for the future of their homelands. The reporters did not inquire what they were doing, how they lived, what they thought about India, what their private discussions were about, or what conditions were like in Africa. They merely summarized the Presidential address and the telegrams of congratulation.

This journalistic tradition of relying on official communiqués is both good and bad. It is bad because the urban intellectual who runs India does not know enough of what happens in the village or the city slums. It means that his attention is drawn more often to failure than to success. The success found in Government communiqués or political speeches is discounted as propaganda. The failures are dramatic news — a famine, a Naga uprising, or the publication of an Estimates Committee Report criticizing a particular Government enterprise. But there are some good aspects of this tradition. There is a certain uniformity of standards; the reader is subjected to a constant trickle of information which tends to move him in one direction, toward progress — more fertilizers, less untouchability, more national unity, less frivolity.

The Indian press, though over a hundred years old, is still young and pompous — pompous because education is the privilege of the few. As more people learn to read and write, they will want the press to write down to their level, and many an austere daily may become a tabloid. The impact of the newspaper is now felt mostly in the towns; in the villages it is still erratic, except in South India, where there is a high degree of literacy.

RADIO

More important to the village than the newspaper is the radio, since it can be appreciated by the illiterate. The radio is not confined to the towns. The Community Projects and the National Extension Blocks are distributing so many dry-cell radios that there is now one within walking distance of perhaps one village in four. With the extension of electricity there will soon be even more radios.

All India Radio is Government-owned, and its programs are never commercially sponsored. It does many things for many people. It provides the cultivator with the latest market price for his produce and thus makes him profit-conscious. It gives him an accurate weather forecast, which is undermining the importance of the 'rain-better,' India's most picturesque character — a sort of bookie on the weather who takes a fee for predicting rain or a commission on betting about rain. It gives the politician a wide audience. It provides the peasant with agricultural tips and with recreation.

The recreational broadcasts are mostly historical or devotional: plays about Indian heroes and gods, devotional music and singing, readings from the Gita and the Ramayana or Bhajans (psalms). Before the coming of the radio, the villager had to wait for an itinerant minstrel or a holy man to recite the holy texts. Once in a great while, such a traveler might spend a couple of days in the village. Everyone would gather to listen to him often until dawn, with children sleeping on their sisters' laps. Now it is enough to turn the little knob on the 'box that makes a noise,' as some call it, and the 'celestial voice' (the Hindi name for All India Radio) will oblige. Devotional songs will pour forth telling of the love of Ram for Sita, of the demon's dark designs on Sita, and of Hanuman's timely assistance.

The radio is both a progressive and a stabilizing influence. On the one hand, it brings the messages of urbanization and technology and further undermines the orthodoxy that urbanization is beginning to destroy. On the other hand, it brings the old religious traditions back to the villages and the towns, so that, strangely enough, both a decline in orthodoxy and a religious revival are going on side by side in India today.

MOTION PICTURES

The influence of the newspaper and the radio is reinforced by the motion pictures. The Indian film industry is the second in the world in footage produced, if not in quality. Judged by Western standards, Indian films are bad. Technically they mostly belong to the days when the Gish sisters drew tears from sophisticated audiences and every woman adored Valentino. Indian acting is melodramatic. Plots are nearly always poor. Too often there is enough plot for five ordinary full-length pictures, and one film lasts from three to five hours. A script is sold on the number of songs and dances it has; it does not matter that they have no continuity. Millions of people will buy ten-cent seats ten times or more, not for the film itself but for the music.

The plots of Indian movies are of three kinds: religious and mythological, historical, or modern. Two thirds of the plots are religious and depict the life of a saint or a god — indeed, many Indians go to the movies as they would to the temple. These films contribute nothing to India's nonviolent revolution.

Typical of historical films, and rather better than most, is the lavish technicolor production *Jhansi Ki Rani*. This is the story of the Rani of Jhansi who lost her life while helping to organize the Sepoy Mutiny. Such films, in their ridicule and criticism of the British, help to build up Indian national pride.

Far more revolutionary are the plots of 'modern' Indian films, which are invariably about 'boy meets girl.' This is dynamite in the Indian world of arranged marriages. Indian films persistently try to undermine the traditional influence of the horoscope. In them the villain woos the heroine (via her father) with the connivance of a court astrologer or a village priest. For a consideration, the priest or the astrologer casts a favorable horoscope, provides a love philter, and prays for the villain's cause. In the end, the villain always fails, and in retaliation he beats up the astrologer and the priest or even kicks the god's image to smithereens. In spite of the horoscope and the priest, the good boy meets the girl and they fall in love. They are never of the same caste or background (otherwise, there would be no film); there can be no Prince Charming but a chimney sweep for a Hindu Cinderella. The girl suffers terrible ordeals inflicted by her orthodox father, who is goaded by the villain and the priest. The father may go blind in protest or, better still, he may set fire to his daughter because she is in danger of losing caste. (Even a Harijan can lose caste — for example, by marrying a caste boy.) Yet, because it is a modern film, the daughter escapes from her father and, if she does not commit suicide because she wrongly thinks herself abandoned by her beloved, she and he marry and live happily ever after.

Few people in India, outside of a few Communist producers, realize how revolutionary films are to India's peasants and workers; most are deceived by their low quality and vast output. But motion pictures are the most effective solvent of untouchability and caste, for neither caste nor creed count in the buying of tickets. The Union Finance Minister, a high-caste South Indian Brahmin, once discovered, during an intermission, that he was sitting next to his own sweeper.

Most Indians go to the movies to hear music and see dances. Yet, insidiously and treacherously, modernization is there — hidden by a familiar song, peering through the painted setting rescued from the attic of a 1900 Brighton photographer, winking at the unmarried girl from under the Chinese bridge on which the heroine pats a paper flower and gushes a complaint. An old clerk in Bihar saw the danger. He explained that he goes to the movies alone, unless the film is on a safe subject like the life of Lord Krishna. 'There can be no hokeypokey of equality or love there. It is all pukka orthodox. I have to think; my daughter is already twelve; soon she will have to be married. One cannot take risks,' said the wise father.

Films, especially the modern ones, make a difference in other ways, too. The young man who sees a beauty on the screen looks more critically at the girl by his side. She, in turn, tries to make the most of what nature gave her. Love on celluloid brings in its wake such consumer goods as plastic combs, brassières, fountain pens, bush coats, Western-cut blouses. The village hut in an Indian film is graced with a chair, perhaps with a mirror or a table, always with a white metal bucket for water instead of the traditional jar, sometimes with such a newfangled gadget as a drinking glass or a fountain pen. These are accompanied by pleasing tunes, which are a cross between American jazz and Hindu ritual chant. Slowly but surely, drinking glasses and buckets are coming to the villages, and chairs are becoming a coveted symbol of affluence. If a man is modern enough, daring enough, and unorthodox enough to sit on a chair and eat from a table, his life has been truly changed. Before the chair came, he squatted on his heels, ate from a banana leaf or a tray flat on the ground, and drank from his hands or from a brass bowl. Now he has stainless steel utensils and eats above the dust. And he has to work harder to pay for these luxuries.

Not all films are revolutionary for good. There are films about Bombay belles, whose lives are wasted by too much pleasure. These films are set in a luxury that clumsily tries to dwarf Hollywood at its most vulgar. They would fan class hatred were it not that the simple-minded public thinks they are as fanciful as fairy tales.

Then, there are the rarer and better films, with a Communist theme, which owe a lot to the ones exported from the U.S.S.R. in the 1930's — grim, class-conscious, well acted, realistic. Typical of these is *Do Biga Zamin* ('Over One Acre of Land'), in which honest and poor tenants are driven out by a rich and greedy landlord who wants to build a mill on his land. Father and son go to evil Calcutta, where the sweat and blood of the poor are drunk by the rich. There, crime lurks around every latrine and every dark alley, and fate and the villain conspire to ruin the innocent villagers. Such a plot is effective indeed for those educated enough to follow it — and therefore able to overlook the fact that there are only three songs and one dance instead of nine of each — but it is completely lost on the masses, who go to the movies to be entertained rather than to learn.

There are also exceptional pictures like *Pather Panchali*, which won the International Award at Cannes in 1956 for the best human documentary. A film of flawless beauty, it is about a village where poverty makes good people bad without their knowing it. But like so many really artistic creations, *Pather Panchali* has been a flop in India outside Bengal. It doesn't have enough action or noise for Indian tastes; only the most modernized of Indian intellectuals appreciate its simple beauty.

A typical example of a mass audience and its reactions was
the Rayalaseema rural open-air show, where the public got
bored with the picture — a cloak-and-dagger Rajput romance
of dubious taste. The crowd scuffled its feet, belched, talked
across heads. Someone in the front row started a quarrel. Two
village groups took sides, and soon the mezzanines were far
livelier than the screen, where a bloody battle between naked
Nagas and Rajput cavalry was raging. The police came; the
row increased, until the nasal voice of the heroine bewailing
in song her destitution did what the constabulary could not.
The uproar suddenly ceased, and silence was followed by
harmony, as all listened to the shrill and nasal scales.

RENAISSANCE

As Western winds blow upon Indian society, an Eastern
wind arises from the heart of India — the village. India, like
Italy after the Middle Ages, is going through a Renaissance.
This Renaissance has yet to mature, but it is here in the wake
of Independence, which is perhaps the best proof of the virtue
of self-government. This Renaissance is all-pervading like
Hinduism. It spans a religious revival and a quite new affection for peasant craft. Only ten years ago, the educated modern Indian kept his religion hidden in a corner of his life;
today he casually and openly goes to the temple and he fasts;
he is no longer on the defensive. Then he always ate with
knife and fork; now, if he feels like it, he eats with his fingers.
The extraordinary strain that keeping up with the West must
have been is startlingly evident at parties in Delhi, where old
friends describe their latest trip to the great South Indian
temples. Before the war they would have vacationed at
France's Côte d'Azur or England's Lake District.

When everyone changes so much, it is hard to remember
how things used to be. Fortunately there are still a few land-
marks of the old ideals of progress. The pretty, foreign-
educated socialite of a decade ago called her friends 'darling,'
dressed in saris of French georgette, read Somerset Maugham,

drank whiskey, went abroad for her holidays, furnished her spacious living room with chintzes from England, kept open house at all hours of the evening, and slept late in the day. Today when she still does so, she is as out of date as she was once progressive; she is a pathetic, lonely reminder of the days when Indians wanted to be Sahibs. Now the educated Indian learns Sanskrit and traditional Indian dancing, joins a classical musical society, wears village cotton saris or her grandmother's saris, of thick silk in gorgeous colors shot through with the glitter of a peacock's tail. A stylish house is decorated not with chintz, but with hand-loomed curtains or tribal rugs, village pottery, bronzes, and old carvings; silver ornaments and ancient enamels replace imitation Cartier jewelry. Now it is important to read R. K. Narayan, the Ramayana, the Mahabharata, and the Bhagavad-Gita.

Thus, the village, 'that little republic,' is returning to the town the best of the traditions it has so jealously preserved for such a long time. The Indian Renaissance is still superficial, but it will grow deep, for its base is broad. East winds, west winds, they all blend to make India one.

10

The Children of God

How did the practice of untouchability arise in India?
Some say it was through religion. Others say it was for the
sake of hygiene. Some say it was custom. Others say it was
color prejudice. Whatever the reasons, the fact is that in
India today there are sixty million untouchables, or Harijans,
as they are called — that is, every sixth Indian is 'impure.'
The raising of these sixty million Indians to a position of
equality with other Indians is one of India's most pressing
problems.

'Impure' does not mean that a person is dirty; a very clean
person may be 'impure.' The touchable Hindu believes that
the untouchable is impure because of sins committed in a
previous life.

The traditional Harijan occupations, however, are dirty in
themselves. The sweeper is obviously untouchable, as are the
scavenger and the tanner; they all handle unclean matter.
The cobbler is untouchable because he handles leather. The
weaver, whose loom in the past had ribs of dead cattle and
gut to hold the warp in place, was also polluted. The fisherman handles fish, dead and alive. The washerman handles
menstrual clothes. The midwife is untouchable because birth
is unclean.

Thus, it is not unreasonable to suppose that the practice of
untouchability may have begun as a hygienic precaution. Not

touching those whose profession involves handling carrion, night soil, and rubbish of all kinds in a damp, hot country like India at a time when soap and germs were unknown was only sensible. It minimized the risks of contagion and reduced epidemics. However, we must remember that in the past impurity could be magical as well as physical. Birth and menstruation produced impurity because they were thought to be magically dangerous.

The practice of untouchability goes back many centuries to the time when laws were made by Brahmins for Brahmins; other people had to accept them unquestioningly. A non-twice born who was caught reciting the Vedas had his tongue cut off. By the time the British came, Indian society was stratified by social custom and by law, particularly in the villages where Moslem influence was small. A Harijan could not pass through a caste street; he could not enter a caste temple or stand next to a caste Hindu. He could not ride a horse or wear silk cloth or ornaments.

The first person to be shocked by the practice of untouchability was the Lord Buddha, some twenty-five hundred years ago. But when Buddhism migrated from its birthplace, India, it left behind magnificent monuments, a chastened Hinduism — and untouchability. In A.D. 52, the Apostle Thomas landed in India and converted some Hindus to Christianity. They retained their caste structure, however, as did Indians who were later converted by the Portuguese in the sixteenth century. From time to time during the years Hindu religious reformers preached equality by personal example, but they had no effect on society. When the Moslems came to India in 1192, they converted many Harijans. These conversions, as was true of the later conversions by Protestant missionaries, had no effect whatsoever on the attitude of Hindu society toward the converted Harijans, who remained outside the pale of Hindu society. The persistence of untouchability among even the most egalitarian of religions illustrates the difficulties in the way of changing an emotional, almost voodoo belief. Some Catholic churches in Southern India have special benches in the rear for their Harijans.

The practice of untouchability was first really challenged when the British courts introduced the concept of complete equality before the law. Up to then, according to old Hindu law, a Brahmin guilty of murder could not be hanged, while a non-Brahmin's hand was chopped off if he had lifted it, even in self-defense, against a Brahmin. Under the British, if a Brahmin wanted to be heard, he might have to stand next to a Harijan petitioner on the officer's veranda, whether it polluted him or not. It was made illegal to cut off the tongues of Harijans or anyone else, and murder — whoever the culprit and whoever the victim — became punishable by death. This was the first blow to caste.

It was Gandhi who really started the campaign to eradicate untouchability. The ideal of equality before the law, together with his Western education, was the background of his campaign. Gandhi was not primarily a politician. As he himself said many times, he was forced into politics by the need to further his experiment with Truth. Gandhi was primarily a social reformer of the Karma Yoga (the yoga of action). A man of action, he was guided by a ruthless regard for the practical. He made the eradication of untouchability one of his principal aims in life. It may even be argued, although it is an oversimplification, that his struggle for self-government was conditioned by his determination to make the Harijan a first-class citizen in every way. The British Government had not interfered in Indian social and religious matters beyond providing equality before the law. Real progress in making the untouchables equal could only be achieved when India was independent.

The first thing that Gandhi did on his return from South Africa forty years ago was to rename the untouchables 'Harijans,' or 'Children of God.' He undertook to lead the life of a Harijan: he cleaned latrines for others as well as for himself; he lived among Harijans and insisted that his followers also live with them. Gandhi thought that the initiative

to do away with untouchability must come from Hindus, because:

. . . untouchability is the sin of the Hindus. They must suffer for
it, they must purify themselves, they must pay the debt they owe
to their suppressed brothers and sisters. Theirs is the shame and
theirs must be the glory when they have purged themselves of the
black sin. The sufferings of thousands of non-Hindus on behalf of
the untouchables will leave the Hindus unmoved. Their blind eyes
will not be opened by outside interference, however well inten-
tioned and generous it may be; for it will not bring home to them
the sense of guilt. On the contrary, they would probably hug the
sin all the more for such interference. All reform to be sincere and
lasting must come from within . . .*

Can untouchability be removed by force? The only way by
which you and I can wean orthodox Hindus from their bigotry
is by patient argument and correct conduct. I am willing to stand
by you, to share your sufferings; you must have the right of worship
in any temple in which members of other castes are admitted. You
must be eligible for the highest office in the land. That is my definition of the removal of untouchability. But I can help you in this
only by following the way indicated by my religion and not by
following Western methods.†

Gandhi's genius was that he never forgot that, in order to
go fast, one must tread cautiously and not arouse the resistance of those upon whose co-operation the success of the
mission depends. Thus, he reassured the caste Hindus:

The orthodox section that disapproves [of the removal of untouch-
ability] is entitled to every courtesy and consideration. Personally,
I am sure that interdining is a necessary reform. I should, however,
resist the attempt to break down the restriction in this in regard
to the feelings of others. On the contrary, I would respect their
scruples in the matter.‡

Interdining and inter-caste marriage are in no way essential for
the promotion of the spirits of brotherhood or for the removal of
untouchability.§

I have absolutely no desire that the temple should be open to

* *Young India*, 1 May 1924.
† Ibid., 22 May 1925.
‡ *My Soul's Agony*, 7 November 1932.
§ *Young India*, 19 March 1925.

the Harijans until caste Hindu opinion is ripe for the opening. It is not a question of the Harijans asserting their right of temple entry or claiming it. They may or may not want to enter that temple even when it is declared open to them. But it is the bounden duty of every caste Hindu to secure that opening for the Harijans.*

Gandhi exhibited his uncanny political wisdom over the issue of separate electorates, an issue that brought him into a headlong fight with the British a quarter-century ago. He entered into a fast unto death in protest against the British intention to create a separate electorate for the Harijans. Gandhi's argument was that the Harijans are Hindus; that, therefore, they must be treated like Hindus, not like Moslems, who already had a separate electorate. The reason for his stand was that, since they are a minority everywhere in India, the Harijans could not afford to become a separate nation, as the Moslems could. The creation of a separate electorate for them would merely have brought about class war within Hinduism itself. But if the Harijans had no separate electorate, adult suffrage would make their welfare the concern of all Hindus.

Now, instead of the separate Harijan electorate desired by the British and Dr. Ambedkar, the first leader of the Harijans from outside Congress, Assembly seats are reserved for Harijans in the areas where they are numerically strong. This reservation of seats works through double-member constituencies. There are two seats: one open to any candidate, the other to a Harijan only; both candidates are elected by everybody. The purpose of reserving seats is to ensure that Harijans will be represented in both Parliament and the State Assemblies in proportion to their percentage in the population. Without such reservations they might not be elected while they are poorer and less educated than other Hindus. But it is a temporary device; as soon as the 'backward' are brought into line, reservation will go. Meanwhile, the movement

* *Harijan*, 23 February 1924–29 April 1933.

toward equality proceeds at the pace of the majority; thus, revolution is watered down into evolution.

The problem of equality has to be approached from various angles — economic, educational, religious, social, and legal.

Harijans are so poor that they can scarcely afford to relinquish their untouchable status. 'We told our Harijans that we were ashamed of the practice of untouchability,' explained the head man of a Deccan village. 'We told them that it was our considered view that we would treat them like caste villagers, allow them to draw water from our well, and eat with us. We said we would bury our own cattle, but of course we would no longer pay them grain for scavenging. The Harijans held a meeting and sent a deputation to say that they wanted to continue to be untouchables because they could not manage without the grain we give them. What are we to do? The Harijans themselves are so poor that they continue to eat carrion and cannot give up scavenging.'

The village Harijan is indeed a victim of poverty. Until the Government gives him land or a job or until he becomes an urban worker, it will be difficult for him to move out of untouchability. Where the Harijan has economic independence or an alternative to his traditional vocation, the abolition of untouchability, backed by education and law, is in sight.

The Government is seeking and adopting every possible means to raise Harijan status. In some States, elected village panchayats must by law include Harijans. In those villages where the Harijans have some economic independence, they actually participate in the Panchayat, and in some cases even the secretary is a Harijan. However, there are still many cases where participation is either nominal, with the Harijans taking no interest in the debates because they know that they will not be listened to, or farcical, as in a Mysore village where they are not even allowed to be present at the discussions but are expected to put an assenting thumb on the dotted line.

The first conscious step on the Harijans' lengthy road to equality is always the opening of schools. As long as they re-

main uneducated, they are contented with their lot, not only
because they believe in the will of God but also because — in
imitation of their 'betters,' the caste Hindus — they have
evolved their own caste hierarchy over the years. They have
over 632 castes and subcastes patterned on the caste Hindu
system with as many rules about mixing and marrying as the
most punctilious of Brahmins. This casteism among outcastes
makes it possible for every Harijan to retain his self-respect by
feeling himself superior to somebody, and also makes it possible for the caste Hindus to exploit the resulting disunity.

The Government of India is spending large amounts of
money on propaganda against untouchability as well as on
means to educate Harijans — by way of grants, scholarships,
and hostels. The educational standards for the admission of
Harijans to college have been lowered, while the age limit has
been raised for government jobs. But education does not work
overnight. Even in England it is said to take two generations
to make a gentleman. In India two generations are not
enough, because intercaste marriage — that ironing board of
Western society — is not so possible. What takes two generations, or nowadays sometimes one in England, still tends to
take three generations in Hindu India. There are exceptions
of course. A number of Harijans have been sufficiently educated, either in colleges or in Gandhi's camps, and have
learned enough of the ways of non-Harijan society to become
fully integrated citizens.

Since the Harijan is a Hindu, conversion is not a possible
remedy. As Gandhi said, 'If a change of religion could be
justified for worldly betterment, I would advise it without
hesitation. But religion is a matter of the heart. No physical
inconvenience can warrant the abandonment of one's religion. . . .' The Harijan is proud of being a Hindu, and he
is a good Hindu.* He does not necessarily want to go to the
Brahmin temple, just as a Low-Church Episcopalian is not

* Except for the Harijan caste of Mahars, Dr. Ambedkar's caste, who are all
converting to Buddhism as a political protest, at their leader's instigation.

eager to attend a High Anglican church; the Harijan may prefer to worship some more popular version of a Sanskrit god. He is quite happy in his religion, and its rituals provide him with a respected status in his village at festival time, since traditional musical instruments can be played only by Harijans. During Hindu festivals, it is the Harijan who plays ritual music. Even in family ceremonies the caste Hindu depends upon him. Music must be played for a girl's first menstruation, and for a death, or a marriage. Where there is a gradual relaxation of the importance of religious ritual, both in the village and in the family, the Harijan gains as a citizen are offset by the loss of a powerful weapon of blackmail, particularly with the advent of modern gadgets. If he refuses to play the flute at young Ramaswami's betrothal, the family can put a record on the phonograph. And for religious festivals there is now the radio.

To achieve equality it is also necessary to make respectable or do entirely away with the traditional untouchable occupations. In the towns, sweepers will remain untouchable as long as the disposal of night soil is not mechanized and as long as they use their hands to sweep and carry refuse on their heads in little wicker baskets which leak. Once the cities have proper lavatories, there will be no sweepers. Fortunately the villages have nature for a latrine. Scavenging is a more difficult profession to deal with because the scavenger not only handles dead animals but also eats their carcasses. Before tanners are accepted they must change their mode of operation; tanning in India is revolting to watch and, since the cobbler works in leather, until a substitute process is found, the prejudice against his profession will remain. The fisherman is caught because there is no escaping from his telltale odor. On the other hand, the weaver has now used wood or metal instead of animal ribs and guts in his loom for so long that he is gradually moving toward respectability. The musician who uses strings made of gut or drums made of hides may have to switch to plastics to become respectable, for it is the material in the instrument, not the music, that is defiling. The musician who uses an earthen pot is touchable. The washerman is slowly on his way out, at least in the towns, where soap and running water, combined with the high cost of cloth, are transforming a profession into another daily chore for the housewife.

The Government has been doing as much as it can to make the Harijans equal in law. For example, temples have been legally opened to them. In Madras, over one thousand of the religious trusts which run all Madras temples have accepted at least one Harijan on their boards. In all states it is a criminal offense to refuse Harijans entry into eating places, shops, public transport, or places of recreation and to refuse to rent to Harijans. And the burden of proof that discrimination was accidental falls on the accused. In addition, each state has at least one Harijan Minister and Harijan legislators in proportion to the percentage of Harijans in the population. There are, in all, 30 Harijan Ministers, 72 out of 500 Harijan members of Parliament, and 564 legislators out of 3356. By 1953, thirty-six acts had been passed to remove social inequalities among Hindus, and a 1955 Central Act made the practice of untouchability a criminal offense all over India.

Laws are not enough. The Government of India is fully aware that it can provide the legal, educational, and social means by which the Harijans can free themselves, but, having done this, it can do no more. The rest must come from the Harijans. Until they are ready to avail themselves of what the Government is doing, they cannot be freed.

The difficulties were brought vividly home to me during a famine in South India in 1952. The monsoon had failed for the seventh time in succession. People were short of drinking water. Wells had gone dry, and in many places the population was reduced to drinking water brought in Army trucks. The Army insisted on giving water first to the Harijans and then to the rest of the village. The Harijans were not pleased by such unsolicited favoritism, for the caste villagers took their humiliation out on them as soon as the Army had turned its back.

I fell into the same error as the Army during that famine. I was taken by a minor official to a series of Government gruel centers. Twice a day, these centers gave free food to anyone prepared to swallow a revolting liquid which swarmed with cooked flies and whose caloric value varied, according to its dilution, between five and eight hundred calories per dollop. The gruel supplemented the diet of the better-off villagers; it was the whole diet of the poor. In one center, there were two separate queues. In one stood well-dressed villagers, metal pots in hand, before a cauldron out of which a village volunteer doled thick porridge. This was the caste queue. In the other queue, ragged creatures, many of whom carried a few leaves made into a cup instead of an earthen pot, waited like prisoners in a concentration camp for a very thin gruel. That was the Harijan queue. I could not help insisting that the queues be switched. As I had expected, the caste queue stared at me with fierce resentment, but to my surprise there was even greater hatred in the Harijans' eyes — hatred mixed with fear.

That evening, I called on the District Administrator, himself a Harijan. He was most unfriendly and, after a few drinks, exploded with anger: 'I have been told of what you have done in the village. Why the hell can't you all, and I mean all, stop meddling and leave us alone? I know you think that because I am an untouchable, I am a coward, that I play up to the caste Hindus and let my own kin starve, that I do not follow the Directive Principles of the Constitution. But are the Directive Principles of the Constitution going to protect the victims of your generous indignation from reprisals tonight by the caste villagers, all of whom have a stranglehold on them? The Harijans owe them money and work for them. If they are thrown out of the village, where will they go?'

Pioneering is never easy. Everywhere there are martyrs to emancipation just as there used to be to religion. I visited the family of a young Harijan in Northern India. A bright boy, he had secured a scholarship to study in the nearest town and he stood first at the end of the year, to the fury of his hostel companions, all of whom were caste Hindus. Instead of showing their fury, however, they celebrated his success by giving him sweetmeats. By the time he arrived home he was deathly ill, with symptoms of poisoning. His father informed the police, who promised to investigate. Before the doctor could be reached, the youth died. Despite police instructions, the parents disposed of his body, thus destroying any evidence. No action could be taken. His widow told me, with tears in her eyes, that she was treasuring all his books. 'For our son when he grows up,' she said, smiling at her handsome baby.

Pioneers are not always killed. A young Harijan administrator lived next door to a merchant's widow in a small town in North India. The widow, who was very poor, had a pretty daughter but no money for her dowry. The merchants of the town would not marry a penniless girl. So the widow encouraged meetings between her daughter and the young administrator — he had position and security even though he was an untouchable — and after a time they fell in love and decided to get married. The town merchants did not object until he told his future mother-in-law that he wanted a marriage ceremony according to the rites of his untouchable community. The widow and the girl did not mind. But merchant respectability demanded that no untouchable procession cross a merchant threshold. If such horrible doings were permitted, where would the world go? Innumerable anonymous letters threatening his life and that of the girl did not deter the groom. He was proud of being a Harijan. So the merchants persuaded the girl's younger brother, a useless hanger-on, to testify in court that the administrator had once attempted to rape his sister. The administrator was convicted in the local court, but later acquitted when he appealed.

This incident indicates how India is changing, for in the old days no Harijan would have dreamed of marrying into a merchant family, just as no merchant community would have been prepared to turn a blind eye to such a *mésalliance*. To-day orthodoxy reasserts itself only when custom is openly flouted.

There will be difficulties for a long time, though, particularly when custom is involved with status. Thus, in Government hostels, nobody minds very much sharing a dormitory with Harijans, as long as the latter keep their distance and do not take water from the common jug, but wait for a colleague to serve them — much as if the jug were a village well. Even in Bombay City, there are still factories where Harijans have to drink from separate taps.

Hindus are prepared to compromise with caste where it suits them. In a Mysore village, there is a temple which no Harijan may enter for worship despite the law against discrimination. Since, however, the temple is also the village school, Harijan children go there in the morning, and the teacher is a Harijan. In the afternoon, the temple is used by the village council, which has two Harijan members. They have to stand outside, ready to put their thumb mark on any document handed out to them by the other members of the council. In the evening, when the building is used for worship, all Harijans must stand outside at the prescribed distance. This seems entirely logical to Hindus, who declare, 'If there can be pollution through touch, why not through space?'

While some caste Hindus compromise for convenience, some Harijans still feel a genuine sense of sin and godly wrath when they break convention. A Rajasthan leatherworker once told me that when he had drawn water from the caste well the week before, the villagers wanted to beat him; they had been stopped in the name of the law by the village accountant. The leatherworker said he now took water from the cattle pond because the well had suddenly gone dry. His old mother, squatting in the yard, added vivid descriptions of how, before the well went dry, 'snakes and worms' had filled it first. When

I inquired further, they admitted that the well had actually gone dry not the week before but three years before. When I talked to the village accountant, he boasted proudly: 'No untouchable would ever dare draw water from our well.' He was right, of course, for Rajasthan is particularly backward. Thus, the Harijan leatherworker's story was pure fantasy, in which his wish to be equal with the caste villagers had been tempered by a proper sense of sin for departing from his station in life.

The law and the machinery of Government is always behind the Harijans, although there will always be cases of caste assertion and intimidation. Educated public opinion is equally on the side of the Harijan when orthodoxy publicly defies the law. For example, when Acharya Vinoba Bhave took some Harijans into a temple from which they were barred, he was beaten up by the priests, and his party was thrown out. With great ostentation, the priests disinfected the temple and performed expensive purification rites. The Government could not ignore such defiance. The chief Minister of the State and members of his Cabinet took a procession of Harijans into the temple and forced the priests to officiate while they were there. How many Harijans now go to that temple? Probably one every blue moon. Nevertheless, with every such incident the resistance of the orthodox slowly weakens. As a Rajasthan villager moaned, 'The Government is mixing the maize with the wheat and the millet. We are helpless.'

The feeling about temple entry was once very strong. To appreciate the progress made by propaganda and law, one must look back to the situation before Independence. In 1938, when my English husband came out to India to join the Civil Service, he was young and innocent. During one of his first visits to a town under his jurisdiction, he accepted the invitation of local leaders to pay his respects to the local deity. He entered the temple barefoot and gave the traditional

rupee to the god. The priest smeared his forehead with red
powder, ghee, and rice and gave him the traditional coconut
shavings to eat. The following week, there was a discussion
in the municipal council: Should the temple be thrown open
to untouchables or should it be shut down forever since it had
been polluted by my husband? The council decided that the
temple could not be opened, even to Harijans because it had
been finally polluted. The decision was not intended to hurt
my husband. Indeed, the lawyer who had advocated closing
the temple was as respectful and friendly as ever the next time
he appeared in my husband's court. Today nobody bothers
about who enters a small-town temple. To purify it, at the
most, a few chants are sung, incense sticks are burned, and
holy water is sprinkled on the ground. However, it is different
in the villages, where change is still to come. Harijans seldom
dare enter caste temples.

I saw an example of the growth of tolerance in two separate
visits to the famous temple of Trimbak, not far from Bombay.
On my first visit in 1952, just as I crossed the outer gate, the
head priest darted out stuttering with indignation, 'Get out
quickly.' He followed me into the street, where we had an
entertaining argument in the purest English. This is more or
less the gist of our conversation:

'Why can't I go in?' I asked.

'Because you [like all foreigners] are an untouchable,' he
replied.

'So what? Haven't you heard of the new laws about untouchability?' I protested. 'I may be an untouchable, but how
do you know that I am not an untouchable Hindu?' I once
knew two Europeans who, after a long initiation in Banaras,
were finally promoted to the dizzy height of Hindu untouchability. Being only two people, they had not been able to
form a new caste and had therefore had to content themselves
with being Hindu outcastes.

The priest was unmoved by my argument. 'You may be an

untouchable Hindu, but no untouchable will enter my temple, Constitution or no Constitution!'

'If Mr. Nehru hears about this, you might go to jail.'

'You can tell Mr. Nehru from me to go to hell. The whole town will back me.' And the priest was right. There was already a five hundred strong and extremely hostile-looking crowd watching us.

Three years later I went back to Trimbak with some English friends. When they expressed a desire to visit the temple, I told them that it would be impossible. To my surprise, the taxi driver, who spoke English, said that there would be no objection to our going. He was right. We were allowed to enter, and who but my old enemy the priest took us around and even gave us a glimpse of the Siva Lingam — the symbol of perpetual creation — in the inner sanctum! He did not appear to recognize me, so I spared him an embarrassing recollection.

In backward Orissa, however, foreigners are still not allowed in the magnificent Linga Raj Temple at Bhubaneshwar and when I argued with the temple authorities that they ought not to judge religion on appearance, they answered indignantly that one cannot 'become' a Hindu because 'Hindus are made.' Had I been a Harijan I could have gone in, but as a foreigner I was prohibited.

In the cities discrimination against Harijans is fast disappearing. It is no longer worth risking jail to assert a caste position which urbanization is rapidly breaking down in any case. There are in every Indian city Brahmin restaurants (they are called 'hotels,' but there are almost no hotels as we know them in India) which are not restricted to Brahmins. The 'Brahmin' designation merely tells orthodox Brahmin customers that the cooking and the serving are done by Brahmins.

In the villages, however, discrimination continues, particularly in what used to be 'Princely' India. In parts of Rajasthan, even today, a Harijan may be killed for walking through a prohibited street, wearing gold ornaments, riding a horse, or even eating sweetmeats. And there are still villages in the deep South, where everyone who is not a Brahmin is treated like an untouchable.

On the whole, however, the law is slowly being enforced. As India becomes more industrial and urban, as the standard of living goes up, and as education does away with the bigotry of the orthodox, the day when the Harijan will be equal is drawing near.

11

Old Water — New Hygiene

India's attitude toward hygiene and cleanliness can only be understood in terms of the distinctions an Indian makes between various kinds of cleanliness — ritual, personal, domestic, and civic.

Ritual cleanliness is much older than hygiene. It is the ritualization by religious and social sanctions of empirical rules of cleanliness, determined in the light of human knowledge at the time of the ritualization. This ritualization was necessary if rules of cleanliness were to be observed. Indeed, many of these ritual concepts make for good hygiene, such as the practice of washing one's hands before eating or after going to the bathroom. To an orthodox Jew, washing his hands is a matter of ritual cleanliness. Thus, while a hygiene conscious person may fail to wash his hands if it is going to be inconvenient to do so, an orthodox Jew will wash his hands no matter how great the inconvenience.

Ritual cleanliness is a prominent feature of a number of societies. Only among Hindus, however, is the concept of ritual cleanliness complicated by the concept of pollution. What is pollution? The Pocket Oxford Dictionary defines 'pollute' as 'to destroy the purity or outrage the sanctity of.'

When pollution exists there immediately arises the question of how it can be overcome. When ritual is not involved, purification is relatively simple. For instance, water is polluted by dirt; to purify it, one can filter it, boil it, or throw it away and wash the glass it was in. At the other extreme, in the Jewish and Moslem religions, purification is not possible. The orthodox Jew or Moslem would feel guilty if he ate pork. He might pray to his God to forgive him, but there is nothing he can do to make him feel he had not eaten the pork.

In Hinduism, it is possible to overcome pollution. In fact, there are elaborate rules for depolluting oneself. Such rules are indispensable, because even the most orthodox and God-fearing unavoidably face pollution every day. For a Hindu, pollution is more complex than it is for a Jew. For instance, the taboo against touching one's wife before her post-menstrual bath is common to both religions. But while the very orthodox Jew will not take the household keys from his impure wife but picks them up from the table where she puts them down, the orthodox Hindu cannot even touch the keys, for the key itself has become polluted by the touch of his impure wife. Thus, in Hinduism objects become polluted by touch or propinquity, and this pollution is maintained through time and distance. Keys polluted by touch months ago will remain polluted until they have been ritually purified. A very orthodox Malabar Brahmin is polluted if a Harijan comes within ninety-six feet of him. In this case, pollution has nothing to do with cleanliness but everything to do with status.

Cleanliness, like beauty, is a matter of convention: there is no such thing as an absolute standard of either. Standards of personal cleanliness or hygiene have always been various and changing. For instance the cleanliness of which we in the West are so proud is very new.

By contrast, for thousands of years, Hindus have been conditioned by ritual to eschew contact with objects which, as Westerners recently discovered, contain germs. Hindus draw a sharp distinction between saliva, which is germ-ridden, and urine, which is not only aseptic but becomes antiseptic when it has fermented, or between human feces, which are full of germs, and cow dung, which is free from harmful germs and has certain cleaning properties.

The Hindu concept of cleanliness is at variance with ours in the West. A Westerner seems very dirty to a Hindu: day after day, he uses the same toothbrush, putting back into his mouth what has come out of it. He eats from plates, drinks from glasses, and uses cutlery which is not his alone and has been used before by others. He removes a spot of dust from his face with a handkerchief moistened with saliva and, more revolting still, he sometimes does the same with his children's faces. In the West, saliva may be used to clean, to keep a strand of hair in place, to tidy eyebrows, and to melt mascara on a brush. Not only does the Westerner spit into a handkerchief but he blows his nose in one, not just once but many times. The Indian spits on the floor and blows his nose through his fingers. There is an old Indian riddle: 'What is it the poor man throws away and the rich man carries in his pocket?' 'A cold!' The dirty Westerner bathes in still water, allowing the dirt from his body to settle back on it. He also washes his clothes and his cooking utensils in dirty water and, with the latest detergents, he doesn't even rinse them! Often, the Westerner uses cologne or talcum powder to conceal the odor of sweat. He wears his clothes over and over again before they go to the dry cleaner. To Indians a Westerner smells bad, particularly in crowds. And that is not all: a Westerner sleeps in the same night clothes for a week at a time. He does not wash his feet before going to bed. He enters the house with dirty shoes. He neither changes into clean clothes nor washes before going into the kitchen, and his cook tastes the food everybody else eats. At the table a Westerner behaves like a pig, helping himself from the common bread with his hands, serving himself cooked food and letting the serving spoon touch his plate, and he eats with his shoes on.

But it is over excrement that the Westerner most revolts the Indian, for the division between the water and the toilet paper civilizations is deeply rooted. 'You people are really dirty,' said a leading Indian politician, as we were discussing Western and Indian customs. 'You use paper. I have tried it and I can tell you that unless you also use water you can never get clean. Yet, you think us dirty because we do not use paper. The ideal, of course, would be to combine the two ways: first, yours and then, ours.'

In India, personal cleanliness is ritualized at two levels: one level for the Brahmin and another for the lower castes. But all castes try, in varying degrees, to imitate the Brahmin — directly if they are the next caste down, or indirectly if they are further removed in the scale of caste.

A Brahmin has to bathe before the sun rises. First, he goes to the field to relieve himself, with his sacred thread twisted around his ear to protect it from getting polluted by dragging into excreta. Then he has to have a ritual bath, for he is now polluted at two levels: his left hand has been polluted with excreta, and by extension his whole body has been polluted. Only after his bath does he take his sacred thread down from his ear so that people may know he is clean and can be approached. Except for the sacred thread to remind him to bathe, the non-twice born acts in much the same way, even though he may take only a token bath and need not wash himself before dawn. Both Brahmins and low-caste Hindus wash their mouths after each meal, but Brahmins are more particular about washing hands and feet before eating. Hindus bathe much more often than Westerners do, though relatively few of them use soap, for soap is a luxury in a poor country. They change their clothes every day if they can afford to and, in theory at least, they never wear the same garment twice without its being washed. If they can afford it, they have an oil bath at least once a month, and they wash their hair in water every time they bathe, though the sophisticated wash their hair perhaps only once a week.

Although Hindus are personally clean, they sometimes shock people in the West. Ritual cleanliness, the cleanliness that has nothing to do with dirt but a lot to do with status, is the cause of this 'shocking' behavior. For example, an official delegation of Indian women who went around Europe recently did not flush the toilet even in first-class hotels. Naturally people complained. Before the Indian women agreed to flush after themselves, the leader of the delegation had to explain that there are no sweepers in the West. It was not that the women were exceptionally fussy; it was only that they were afraid that touching the chain would pollute them. And when the Taxation Enquiry Commission met in a modern Bombay building, two women had to be hired to pull the toilet chain between users because the officers would not touch a chain that a sweeper touches at least once a day when he cleans the premises.

There are no sweepers in the villages because there are no latrines. When people go to the fields they take a little pot of water with them. Ritual forbids them to pollute the river bed or the well site; they must be at least forty paces from the source of water. In the old days, it was a crime punishable by death to break the forty-pace rule, but recently, especially in the less orthodox North, many people have come to use the river bed and the well site as they would the field.

The flushing of night soil involves the breaking of the taboo against polluting water — a taboo so strictly enforced that Gandhi was excommunicated for crossing the ocean to go to England. That was many years ago; today this taboo is not so rigid and the Indian who returns from overseas purifies himself by swallowing a token pill made of the five products of the cow — milk, clarified butter, curds, urine, and dung. Flushing night soil is seldom necessary, though, for there is no flush in the village or the small town, where people use the street or, if they are wealthy, have sweepers and commodes. Because the West has long benefited from Sir John Harrington's noble invention, the toilet, we Westerners forget what our towns must have been like when people emptied their chamber pots into the street as a matter of course. Indians at least do not chance polluting passers-by.

To the Westerner, night soil and urine are excreta much
of a kind, to be deposited in the same place. To the orthodox
Hindu they are vastly different. Urine is not polluting, but
night soil is. Urine is part of everyday life. Its all-pervading
stench does not disturb the urbanized Indian, if he notices
it at all. People in India pass water everywhere; village women
use the floor of the courtyard, where the aroma is lost in the
more acrid smell of the cattle's urine. In the cities, too, urine
is not deposited only in certain places. Many orthodox Hindus
do not pass water in the toilet, even if they happen to have
one, but rather on the bathroom floor, which has a little hole
provided for washing it down. Thus, they carry to a logical
conclusion the distinction between pollution and excretion,
for using the toilet would pollute them and necessitate a ritual
bath.

The Government is making great and so far not very successful efforts to make villagers latrine-minded, at least in the
Community Project areas. As the sewage system is being introduced into towns, flushes are becoming gradually more
common. The real difficulty of improving sanitation is the
city slums. Clearing slums is very expensive, particularly when
money and building materials are required for new developments. In an expanding economy like India's slum clearance
is more easily wished for than done.

There is another form of ritual cleanliness that touches on
black magic, although there are good sanitary explanations
for it. That is the belief, common to old-fashioned societies,
that women are impure during their menstrual periods, because they are then vulnerable to evil. In India, this belief
provides the woman with the only rest she ever gets; during
her polluted days, she stays outside the kitchen and rests —
in fact, she does absolutely nothing. At least that is what happens in theory. In practice, if she is needed on the field, she
goes, but she does not have to grind flour or squat over the
smoking fire in the kitchen. Also, after a confinement, the
entire household is polluted for ten to eleven days, during

which, in theory, nobody must come near the family. This is an excellent rule of hygiene, but usually it is not observed, for all the villagers are curious to see a new baby and are willing to sprinkle a drop or two of water on themselves afterward in token purification. Only the pollution of death is fairly rigorously observed. The dying are taken out of the house to die; if they die inside, an elaborate purification ceremony has to be performed. In any case, the family of the dead is polluted for a certain number of days.

Civic cleanliness is practically unknown in India. In this country of villages, every town is new. In most towns, there are people who behave as if they were still in their villages, where nature takes care of many things. They urinate on staircases, spit upon walls, use the streets as garbage cans. In fairness to them, it should be said that this is only partly their fault. In 1953, the city of Calcutta, with a population of close to five million, had only a few dozen municipal urinals and not one thousandth of 1 per cent of the required number of garbage containers. It will take a long time — or totalitarian methods — for Indian cities to become clean.

Where ritual personal cleanliness is great, domestic cleanliness is lacking, because the cleaner one must remain the less one may handle dirt, even to remove it. Only the completely polluted Harijan may really get down to scrub the floor of his house if he wishes. Thus, domestic cleanliness is incredibly spotty in India because it falls between personal and ritual cleanliness. Under village conditions, personal and ritual cleanliness combine to keep the hut clean. People wash themselves; they cow-dung their house with ritual regularity, perhaps not when it is dirty but when the calendar demands it or when there is a slight discoloration of the mud walls — at any event frequently enough to keep the hut clean. The few dishes they own are kept ritually clean; each member of a household cleans his own.

Some Westerners find it hard to adjust to the fact that cow dung and mud are used in India as soap is in the West. Cow dung is no more revolting to a Hindu villager than good wholesome manure is to a peasant in the West. For example, a French peasant has a manure heap just behind his house, level with the kitchen door; he handles it quite casually even after it has fermented and smells. The Indian peasant handles fresh cow dung diluted in water with equal casualness. I have eaten many a meal in freshly dunged rooms and slept many a night on a freshly dunged mud floor. There is a certain cool, medicated cleanliness to the smell of dung and mud which drives away ants and is reminiscent of phenyl. But for the ritual smearing of dung and mud, huts would not be cleaned at all.

In the city, however, the rules of personal and ritual cleanliness did not anticipate all the trappings of urbanization which need to be cleaned — from window panes and doors to furniture — and which are unknown in the village. Marble and wooden floors cannot be cow-dunged. The Indian in transition — no longer living in his village yet still rural in his outlook — runs into difficulties when he applies his old standards of cleanliness to a modern apartment on the fashionable Bombay waterfront or to a spacious bungalow in Delhi. The household chores are left to servants, who are the poor from the village. It is seldom possible to train them to keep things properly clean, for the mistress of the house cannot touch the floor or clean the toilet; she cannot even touch her sweeper or his implements to show him what to do. If she does her own cooking, the kitchen is clean not merely because she is there but because ritually it must be clean. The refrigerator, however, is often dirty, because the materials it is made of cannot be cleaned in the traditional fashion. Moreover, its shape is somewhat baffling. The bathroom may not be clean, for it is a place of pollution. Because Indians wash in running water, the bathtubs are merely used to put a wooden plank in them upon which one stands while pouring water over one's self. The tub itself may not be cleaned for considerable periods. The wash basin is not used as it is in the West. The plug is usually missing, because the wash basin is a place for water to run through, not a container of water. It, too, is only occasionally cleaned, since it never comes into contact with anything. In the less sophisticated houses window panes and doors may be cleaned perhaps once a year, when the walls are re-whitewashed and the dirt on the door painted over. Dirt on doors and windows is of no importance, since the only important thing is personal and ritual cleanliness.

The Government and various agencies, from missionaries to World Health Organization teams, have been trying to bring hygiene to town and country alike. They have not yet achieved enough to make much difference in India as a whole, except in the field of preventive medicine — disinfecting walls, spraying huts with D.D.T., and teaching women and children how to keep flies away. Before people can adopt hygienic living, they must be educated to it and must have both leisure and proper facilities to make cleanliness easy. This is particularly true in a large city like Calcutta, with practically no middle-class amenities. Two thirds of the population live on less than six dollars a week, a pittance which has to keep as many as five people alive. Over 150,000 people sleep on the sidewalks, drink and wash from water hydrants, and have no belongings. And even the relatively prosperous Indians who enjoy modern living have their problems.

Transition is always difficult: people are faced with new circumstances for which the old wisdom no longer provides, and if they take to the new too quickly, the change may be superficial and unsatisfactory. Because Indians think in terms of ritual cleanliness rather than hygiene, they often misunderstand Westerners' attitude toward them.

Comparisons of cleanliness are always invidious. Nothing is more annoying to individuals or more damaging to international relations than one nation feeling it is cleaner than another. This feeling is based on statistical data of how many baths there are per person per nation or tons of soap; it inevitably translates itself into contempt, no matter how unwarranted, and contempt leads to arrogance.

Obviously, where cleanliness is ritual, it lags behind the highest standards of modern hygiene and sets up barriers to the adoption of new methods and customs. Slowly and steadily, however, progress is being made. People are beginning to think in terms of hygiene rather than of ritual. Soon yet another major prop of the old order will begin to crumble.

12

The Minorities

Many people think that India is populated only by Hindus. Yet, there are fifty-nine million Indians who are not Hindus. Of this fifty-nine million the great majority are Moslems. The rest are Christians — most of whom are Roman Catholics — Sikhs, Parsis, Buddhists, and Jews.

THE MOSLEMS

The thirty-seven million Moslems in India — two million more than there are in West Pakistan — constitute India's greatest minority problem. To understand the Indian Moslem, one must go back to 1946, before India was partitioned into India and East and West Pakistan.

The Moslems of undivided India were unable to forget that they had ruled half of India before the British came. They did forget, however, that although they had ruled nearly all of India at one time or another, they had never ruled more than two-thirds at one time, and that the British had taken India more from the Hindu Mahrattas and from the Sikhs than from Moslem rulers. The Moslem resentment over glory lost became acute under the British, because the Hindus were the first to take advantage of English education and government jobs. Soon the Hindus were prospering in the new occupations Westernization had brought, while the Moslems were not. Most of the clerks, doctors, lawyers, and engineers were Hindu. With industrialization, Indians became cotton and jute kings. Very seldom did the Moslems share in this new industrial wealth.

The decline of Moslem power was largely the Moslems' own fault. They did not attach enough importance to education and preferred to stay on the land instead of going into industry. But naturally they blamed the Hindus for the decline in their fortunes. Educated Moslems began to feel that the only way to escape Hindu domination was to have a land of their own. The closer Indian independence came to realization, the stronger became the Moslem desire for their own independence. Naturally this desire was not acute in such areas as Sind, where the Moslems were in a majority, or in areas where they were in a small and prosperous minority as in much of the South. It was sharpest in areas like the United Provinces (now Uttar Pradesh), where the scales between the religions were more evenly balanced. Here the Moslems were a large minority, their tradition of past power was strong, they had culture and position and were treated well by the British. Nonetheless they were still losing ground.

Even so, most Moslems did not favor partition in the years just before Independence. Instead, they wanted to be treated as equals rather than as a minority. They wanted statutes to guarantee them a half share in political power. It remained for the genius of Mr. Jinnah to unify the different strands of frustration, uncertainty, desire for power, the feeling of separateness and superiority of the Moslems into the demand for a separate state: Pakistan. By 1946, when elections were held to determine how large a stake each party would have in the new independent India, Jinnah's Muslim League was a force to be reckoned with. Oddly enough, a large percentage of Moslem votes for the league in that election came from territories which remained in India after the partition.

As soon as the British handed over power, the subcontinent was duly divided. East Bengal, with a population of twenty-eight million Moslems and twelve million Hindus, became

East Pakistan; and at the other end of India, West Pakistan was formed from the Moslem Provinces of Sind, the North-West Frontier Province, Baluchistan, and the Moslem majority half of the Punjab. When India agreed to Partition, it was with the understanding that Hindus would remain in Pakistan and Moslems in India, and that both sides would honor their minorities and treat them as full citizens. That was Mr. Jinnah's desire, too. But, unfortunately tempers had got out of hand by the time India was divided.

The communal riots began in Calcutta in August 1946; they culminated in the frightful civil war in the Punjab in 1947. In Calcutta, after two days of riots in which Moslems killed Hindus, Sikh drivers and Hindu students joined to retaliate. In the week that it took for the re-establishment of law and order, perhaps as many as 30,000 people were killed. Gutters and drains were choked with dead bodies, and people returning to their mansions in the suburbs became so callous that they drove over bodies, dead or alive.

The climax of the violence came in the Punjab at the time of Partition, when perhaps 250,000 people were killed and fifteen million people moved bullock, cart, and family to the other side of the border in the greatest exodus of all history. To make matters worse, in 1948 the Hindus were frightened out of Sind, where there had been no violence. Even today in East Bengal, Hindus are still made so unwelcome that they have been known to leave for India at the rate of 20–50,000 a month. So far over four million have made the move.

Indians realize that, in many ways, they are better off as a result of Partition. They do not want Pakistan back. An Indian Federation with 112 million Moslems, instead of 57 million, and with half the seats and the jobs at the Center reserved for Moslems — the Muslim League would have agreed to no less — would have been quite unworkable. There would have been endless deadlocks at the Center, endless demands by the Moslem majority States for more money. Conditions would have continued as they were from 1946 to 1947 under the joint Muslim League-Congress Cabinet, when the Moslem ministers regarded themselves as custodians of Moslem interests rather than as fellow members of one Indian Cabinet. As I observed at the time, little was accomplished amid the constant quibbling, and a disproportionate amount of bitterness piled up. It would have been even more difficult to get co-operation after Independence because of the different social ideas of the Congress Party and the Muslim League. The Congress Party was led by professional men; its objectives were socialistic. The Muslim League was led by landlords; it was quite happy with the social *status quo*.

Even on a personal level Hindus would have suffered from continued co-existence with such a large Moslem minority, because Islam proselytizes aggressively and is actively contemptuous of idolatry. On the other hand, Hinduism sees truth in all faiths, and Hindus are quite willing to worship at the tombs of Moslem saints, as well as those of their own. Faced with what is to them a fanatic religion, the Hindus have reacted like a garden turtle when it is tortured: it draws its head, tail, and paws back into its shell. In self-defense, during the centuries of Moslem domination of parts of India, Hindus turned introspective; caste stratification acquired new force and rigidity, and Hindus adopted an attitude of indifference toward their rulers, an attitude that is perhaps more exasperating to a government than open rebellion. The more the Hindus turned inward, the more the Moslems bullied them. It was a circle that grew ever more vicious until Partition broke it. Hindu indifference continues even today. It is directed toward the Moslems who remain in India, and the Moslems fear this indifference more than they do persecution.

The basis of Indian acceptance of Partition was that areas might secede on economic, historic, and geographical grounds; it was never that Moslems are Pakistanis first and not Indians. The Congress Party has always insisted that Moslems are Indians, just as Hindus are, and that therefore they must be treated exactly like other Indians. It was not an easy policy to enforce when the horrors of Partition were vividly before everybody's eyes. Yet, it is to the credit of the Congress Party leaders and of the basic tolerance of the Indian people that the Moslems have not suffered in the parts of India not actively affected by Partition.

To say the Moslems did not suffer is perhaps an understatement. They did suffer fear of the Hindus and economic discrimination. They had reason to fear the Hindus, for they felt that they had betrayed India by voting for the Muslim League before Partition. Moreover, the tension of the last few years before Partition had made them suspect in the eyes of their Hindu neighbors. This suspicion was sometimes translated into economic discrimination. For instance, a Moslem businessman — and many Moslems in India are engaged in wholesale and retail business — might find that his credit, even with a British bank in Bombay, had dropped considerably. The bank was interested not in his religion but in its own security: a Moslem who might at any time migrate to Pakistan was obviously a poor business risk.

Officially, the Government makes no distinction between Hindus and Moslems. The few Moslem civil servants and Army officers who opted for India have done very well — quite as well as their Hindu contemporaries. Today the chief of the Military Academy is a Moslem; there are two Moslem Ministers at the Center; the Chief Justice of Bombay is a Moslem. There are Moslem ambassadors and secretaries to Governments, and a fair proportion of the Ministry of External Affairs is staffed with Moslems.

The reasons for India's policy of secularism are varied. There is a practical reason, which the late Sardar Patel (deputy Prime Minister and Home Minister between the years 1947 and 1950) explained to me at the height of the 1950 riots.

'We must protect our Moslems, come what may — even if it means shooting a lot of Hindus. We might argue that if we do not protect our Moslems, they will move to Pakistan and we will be better off. But, of course, that is a fallacious argument. There is no room for the Moslems of India in Pakistan. They know it, and Pakistan will be quite ruthless. Therefore, to drive the Moslems out, many would have to be killed and we would be left with a nation of criminals. Once a man has tasted blood, he can no longer be a good citizen. Therefore, we shall force our Hindus to behave.'

There are, in addition, the intellectual and moral reasons for secularism that fire Nehru. A man of the world, Nehru was brought up in the gracious atmosphere of the Moslem Zamindars of Uttar Pradesh. He is genuinely secular; he believes in the equality of all people. Sardar Patel once said in jest, 'Jawaharlal is the only Nationalist Moslem.' (The Nationalist Moslems were opposed to the Muslim League in India.)

The moral reason for which Nehru has made the Moslems his own children is perhaps more valid than his intellectual reason. The agnostic Prime Minister of India considers Islam a dam against orthodox, obscurantist Hindu revivalism — a revivalism that haunts his most private thoughts. Has Nehru good reason for this fear? Emotionally and subjectively he does. He has seen Hindus commit the most ghastly murders in the name of religion. Of course, the Moslems have killed as many; indeed, they started it all. But Nehru was more affected by what the Hindus did: he saw the killings in India (by Hindus and Sikhs); he did not see what happened to Hindus in Pakistan. Moreover, Pakistan morals are not in his keeping. And, when a Hindu fanatic murdered Mahatma Gandhi because he was too pro-Moslem, Nehru was finally convinced that Islam must be protected in order to save Hinduism from itself. But, as has been mentioned, indifference and not fanaticism is the distinguishing trait of Hinduism toward other religions. Therefore, from an objective point of view, Nehru would seem to be doing Hinduism an injustice.

Finally, there are political reasons for India's secularity. The Hindus remaining in East Pakistan might receive even worse treatment if India pushed her own Moslems about. As long as India wants Moslem Kashmir to prefer union with India to union with Pakistan, Moslems in India must be treated as full citizens.

However, these two reasons are secondary, and indeed temporary, compared with the necessity for India to be secular that comes from her geographical and economic place in the world. India is located between Islam and Communism. To the North are Russia and China. Near by are the largely Moslem states of Iran, Afghanistan, Indonesia, Malaya, and, farther west, not only Egypt but the whole of Moslem Africa. Most of the Afro-Asian people are Moslems. In most of these Moslem countries the weakening of Western Europe has left or is leaving a vacuum. Many Indians feel that India should fill this vacuum with her wisdom rather than Russia with her terror or America with her materialism. If India is to influence Moslems in other countries, the Indian Moslem must be treated like a full citizen and his fate must be such as to inspire his brothers in less developed lands.

But these are reasons of *Realpolitik* which, while they may have occurred to her leaders, have not penetrated to the masses. If Moslems are not persecuted or even discriminated against in India, the real reason is not political expediency, but the basic tolerance of the Hindus—their readiness to live and let live as long as they, too, are left alone.

How have the Moslems reacted to being reduced to a minority at the mercy of the majority's good will? The reaction has differed of course, but at first most Moslems had their confidence severely shaken, especially in areas where their authority had previously been unquestioned. How unquestioned this authority could be was expressed by a Hindu friend of mine. He told me that, when he was a boy, he had to step from the sidewalk into the street when a rich Moslem went by and that his father had to dismount from his horse when he passed a Moslem landlord on country lanes.

In 1950 I spent an evening in a city where the Moslems had been powerful only a few years ago. That evening the head of the local Moslem community had invited me and a representative group of Moslems to dinner. The shutters of his huge mansion were drawn; heavy hangings of rich brocade guaranteed our privacy. We talked late into the night. My host was a lonely old man whose children had left him to make new lives in Pakistan. He groped for words to express his sentiments on the new order:

'I have always considered myself an Indian. I refused a very high office in Pakistan because I was born here, my wife is buried here, and this is where I shall die. I built this big house, thinking that in my old age it would ring to the laughter of many grandchildren. Now I am trapped. I cannot sell this house because my loyalty to India would at once be suspect. I cannot visit my children because my property would be confiscated. [The law had since been changed and a man is no longer an 'intending evacuee' if he goes to Pakistan on a visit; and his property is no longer frozen by the state.] If my children visit me more than very occasionally, people will begin to say that I am a spy.' He had never taken any interest in politics. He lived with his books and his work. Now he was waiting to die.

In their worry and apprehension, he and his friends reminded me very much of European Jews in 1938:

'Do you think that we shall be safe?'

'How are we to marry off our daughters when all the eligible young men have gone? We are loyal Indians, but no one in India will trust us.'

'How can we trust Hindus when they are waiting like vultures to pounce on our property?'

'We have no choice. We must trust them. There is no Promised Land for us. There is not even any room in Pakistan.'

Moslem confidence is gradually being restored, however.

Time is a great healer. Both Hindus and Moslems are beginning to forget the heated days when Mr. Jinnah was can-
vassing for Pakistan with a green flag, and many Indian Moslems are as devoted to their country as Pakistanis are to theirs.

Several years ago, I was having lunch with an Indian Moslem and a visiting relative from Pakistan. Their conversation
drifted to the position of Moslems in India.

'I am sorry for you,' said the Pakistani. 'You have to educate your children in Sanskritized Hindi, and Urdu is dying.'

'What rubbish!' answered the Indian. 'Urdu is not dead.
What about our newspaper? Is it not in Urdu? And Urdu is
taught as a second language in my children's school.'

'Mark my words, it will not last long. And from what I read
in Pakistan, your mosques are falling into disrepair and people
are afraid to protest.'

'Why don't you go and have a look for yourself instead of
reading this silly propaganda? And we at least have no po-
groms of Moslem sects as you had not so long ago, when half
Lahore City went up in flames.'

'We may have our religious differences, but you have communal riots. Why, the other day, I read that five people who
slaughtered a cow for the Moslem New Year were killed.'

'Maybe there was a stray case of rioting, but that does not
mean that we are oppressed. On the contrary, it shows that
we are beginning to feel so much a part of the country that
once again — and to my mind, quite wrongly — we are
flaunting Hindu customs in our misguided pride. In any case,
it is wrong of you to object to the ban on slaughtering cows
when in Pakistan it is impossible to eat pork. I have American
friends who tell me they come across to India for a breakfast
with bacon.'

'Well, after all, Pakistan is a Moslem country. Everybody
in Pakistan is a Moslem. Why should people eat pork? But
in India it is quite different. There are many non-Hindus,
who eat beef.'

'That may be, but it is discourteous of them. We are Indians and, just as the Hindus give up making noise in front of our mosques at prayer time, we must give up killing cows in deference to them.'

'You think you are safe today because you have a good job but, believe me, the moment Nehru is no more you will all find yourselves in the gutter. There will be no Moslems in any but the lowest positions, and you will be jolly glad for Pakistan, where you can marry your daughter safely.'

The Indian Moslem exploded: 'What an ass you are! We shall get the jobs we deserve in competition with others, and that is as it should be. If we are any good, we shall do well. Indeed, you must have a very poor opinion of Moslems to think that it is only Nehru who gets us our jobs. Let me tell you something, and I hope that both of us will live long enough to see it come true. The Indian Moslems will become the most advanced of all the Moslems because, unlike the Moslems of Pakistan or Egypt, they will have to stand on merit, in competition with Hindus. And competition is a healthy thing. As you were telling me before lunch, the standard of the young recruits to the Pakistan administration has already gone down, because there is no longer competition with people on the intellectual level of the Brahmins.'

When the Moslems who voted for the Muslim League and the generation of Hindus who lost life and property with Partition have died, religion in India will be largely a matter of individual conscience and not a political issue. Already the Moslems who consider themselves aliens in India are in the minority. As time goes on — and barring a war with Pakistan — the Indian Moslems will become Indians first, Moslems second. They will be a minority, conscious of their religious and social differences from the majority, but, above all, Indian citizens.

THE CHRISTIANS

The history of Christianity in India goes back nineteen centuries to the Apostle Thomas, who brought the teachings of Christ to South India and who in fact died there. Since then, many different Christian sects — Syrian Roman Catholics, Syrians of the Latin rite, and all the varieties of Protestants — have been established in the South, which was long the maritime crossroads to China. The 8,500,000 Christians in India today live mostly in the larger cities, the South, and the tribal areas.

Most of the five million Roman Catholics in India are the offspring of Hindus who were forcibly converted by the Portuguese. They live along the coasts of Malabar and the Konkan. The source of their conversion can be found in their names, for their ancestors took the name of the priest or the soldier who converted them. The Roman Catholics whose ancestors were converted by preaching usually kept their Hindu surnames: Marie Iengar or Peter Krishnaswami, not Peter Alverez or Marie da Costa. A genuine convert who belonged to a low caste, however, usually took a Biblical name for his surname and became Peter Jacob or Marie Nazareth.

Most of the Catholics in India have one thing in common: they never forget the caste from which they originated, and they always marry back into that caste. In the South there are a few Syrian Christians whom the Apostle Thomas converted from high-caste Brahmins. Not only do they consider themselves Brahmins of Christian denomination, but their women wear their saris back to front, with the pleating behind, so that they may not be mistaken for Brahmin Iengars who were converted to Christianity by a lesser preacher.

Except for those in the French and Portuguese possessions, the Indian Catholics were never powerful, since the rulers were not Catholics. Therefore, they had no great problem of assimilation after Independence. Their problem is only whether to wear shorts and dresses, or traditional unstitched clothes. They had no political or economic power to lose. Indian Catholics are more modern than the Hindus, the Moslems, or the Parsis: they eat practically anything and with anybody, their women work, they marry for love. Such agitation as there has been against Catholic missionaries has been of a political rather than a religious nature. Some Indians have felt that Catholicism has substituted Western for Indian values even in nonreligious spheres. Some politicians object to the conversion of aboriginals and Harijans, who are, of course, voters. Their objection is not religious, but practical: a politician does not like his constituents to have an outlook different from his own.

Indian Protestants do not differ as conspicuously as the Catholics from the surrounding Hindus. They are much fewer in number and far more scattered. They are also divided into a great variety of denominations, from Seventh Day Adventists to High Church Anglicans. They have not changed their surnames and they wear the national dress of their area. Furthermore, they take much more easily to the general Indian ways of neutralism, family planning, birth control, and political thinking. The problem of their assimilation is practically nonexistent.

There is, however, among Indian Protestants a small community, numbering only 112,000, for whom the problem of assimilation has been extremely serious. These are the Anglo-Indians, and their influence in British India was quite disproportionate to their numbers.

An Anglo-Indian is the child or descendant of a British father and an Indian mother; perhaps a British soldier or an engine driver or a police sergeant married an Indian Christian girl; or a tea planter, condemned by the rules of his company to a long spell of bachelorhood, married a pretty aborginal tea cropper. The children of an Indian father and a British or European mother were never considered Anglo-Indians. Their father usually belonged to the professional or landed aristocracy in India and met his European wife while studying abroad. His wife and their children were accepted into his family. These children were Indian in every way; the British may have looked askance at them but they became a part of Indian society.

The Anglo-Indian's case was quite different. They were all too often, and quite unwarrantedly, despised by British and Indian alike. They were not accepted by the Indians because all their standards were British; they were not accepted by the British because they were usually from the lower middle class, while the British in India were mostly of the upper middle class. Until recently, this gap was hard to bridge even in England, and even without the prejudice against color.

Before Independence, it was the ablest Anglo-Indians — the clever men who aspired to higher posts, the pretty women who sought a good marriage — who were discriminated against. The ordinary Anglo-Indians gradually found their level as local recruits in jobs reserved for them and led contented lives. The less talented were permitted to remain in the posts which had brought their ancestors to India. For example, they had a special place in the Central services and the police.

The hardship of being half-caste fell most heavily on the Anglo-Indian woman, who was often so exquisitely beautiful that she was assured of the hatred of women and the love, though not always the chivalry, of men. This was particularly so because she was caught between tastes above her station in life and the ruthless social boycott enforced upon the young subaltern of a good regiment or the clerk in a respectable bank who might have the temerity to marry her. Even in the Indian civil service, where every eccentricity was encouraged, marriage to an Anglo-Indian could mean years in a bad district; it is said that some bad districts depended for good administration on the good looks of Anglo-Indian girls.

The severe strain of being Anglo-Indian in those days distorted many a woman's life. There used to be no worse slander than to call a woman 'Anglo.' Spanish, French, and Italian grandmothers were invented to explain blue-black hair, full lips, those admirable Indian eyes and tapering fingers, but all in vain — a *mem-sahib* could always tell. And in British India, the *mem-sahib* was a real social force. One of the most

extreme cases was that of a senior official who divorced his
wife immediately when an accident made public the fact that
she was not French but Anglo — although *he* had known
it all along.

The status of the Anglo-Indian improved when power
passed from the British to the Indians. It has always been the
Anglo-Indian's difficulty that India was his country. After
Independence, those Anglo-Indians who did not feel this
loyalty went to Britain or Australia, where they were quickly
employed and absorbed. Those who remained in India were
often particularly well qualified to take the place of the
departing British. Today Anglo-Indians are colonels, collectors
of customs, superintendents of police, or district officers on the
railways; in 1947 they were sergeants, warrant officers, and station masters. Under British rule the best of them were discriminated against and the worst of them protected; now,
there are plenty of opportunities for the best.

At Independence the Anglo-Indians were given special
guarantees by the Constitution. They were entitled to special
representation and to employment in the railways, the customs, and the post office; their schools were given special
grants-in-aid for ten years, provided they take 40 per cent of
non-Anglo-Indian pupils; the Commissioner for Scheduled
Castes and Scheduled Tribes was made responsible for their
welfare.

They deserve these privileges, for India owes them much.
They are one of India's most advanced groups. They provide
India with many of its best qualified public officials and
employees in private businesses. They are used to doing all
the jobs that the British and the upper-caste Hindus deemed
below their dignity; their technical know-how helped make
Independence successful.

As the privileges and the discrimination go, the Anglo-
Indians will spread out in India's life as a whole. The least
able may become seamen, laborers, even beggars; the best
may become military commanders or general managers in

the railways. Already the Anglo-Indian woman is fully part of society. The pretty Delhi brides of foreign diplomats no longer have to worry about the ancestor who blackened her curls like a raven's wing, for now nobody cares.

THE SIKHS

There are six million Sikhs, most of whom are concentrated in the Punjab and Delhi. They are famed abroad for their superb physique, their magnificent war record, their beards, and their turbans. In India itself, they are known for bodily strength, gargantuan appetites, considerable mechanical aptitude, enterprise, skill at farming, wooden-headedness, and eager pursuit of women.

The Sikhs are best understood if they are considered a sort of Protestant Hindu brotherhood. They are a militant sect whose origin is traced to a Hindu saint named Guru Nanak, who lived at the end of the fifteenth century. Guru Nanak preached love and the equality of man, irrespective of caste or creed; but soon after his death his religious heirs — he had appointed a successor — began to shift the emphasis from love to war. By the time Gobind Singh, the tenth and last Guru, died, he had made the Sikhs into a formidable guerrilla group in revolt against the oppressive Moghuls. Anybody could join them by adding Singh ('lion') to his name and by observing the many do's and don'ts of the brotherhood. Among the key requirements for the sect are the 'five K's': Kesh (long hair and beard), Kaccha (short underpants), Kankan (a comb symbolizing that the Sikhs were women as long as Delhi was in the hands of the Moghuls), Kirpan (a dagger), and Kangha (a steel bangle, which reminded them of Moslem subjugation). There are also rules against smoking and drinking. The Sikhs do not take the ban on drinking very seriously, for they are known all over India for their addiction to spirits.

Unlike Hindus the Sikhs are 'a people of the Book.' Their book is the Granth Sahib, in which are recorded the teachings of their Gurus. Hindus and Sikhs have lived together without trouble. Sikhs marry Hindu girls, and, although Sikhs may not worship images, all the Hindu gods are named in the Granth Sahib. Indeed, until a few decades ago, the Hindu pantheon was physically represented in the Golden Temple at Amritsar, the holy of holies of the Sikhs.

The Sikhs were cherished by the British whom they served loyally. The British rewarded them with the best of the Punjab's land, which the Sikhs brought into cultivation. However, most of their old land is now in Pakistan. The Sikhs suffered more than any other group from Partition, for they lost their canal colony lands and their Lahore houses and got in exchange, on the Indian side of the Punjab, less than they had left in Pakistan, simply because there was less to go round. It has been calculated that this small community of six million lost as much as nine hundred million dollars in the exchange. Nevertheless, the hardy toughness that has taken Sikhs to California to grow fruit, to Canada to raise minks, or to Calcutta to drive taxis has helped them to make the best of the poor land they were given. As a community they have been the first to recover from the shocks of Partition.

The problem of their assimilation is not religious; people go in and out from Hinduism to Sikhism, and many families have one Hindu and one Sikh brother. Their problem is economic. When the British left, the Sikhs not only lost their patrons but were left somewhat conspicuously more Westernized than other Indians. They are, however, already finding their place, as India's budding industrialization brings them full employment. Also, as the old rituals disappear in India, the Sikhs will become more akin to everyone else. Soon they will be fitted completely into the pattern of the new India.

THE BUDDHISTS

India gave the Buddha to the world twenty-five hundred years ago. Buddhism flourished in India as a reaction against corrupt Hindu practices, much as Protestantism began as a reaction against corrupt Catholicism, and it soared to great heights under Emperor Asoka. Then Hinduism reacted by purifying itself; like quicksand, it reabsorbed the Buddhists of India. At the same time as the message of the Buddha was radiating all across Asia, Buddhism was rapidly dwindling in India itself. As its own priests in India became corrupted, Buddhism was no longer sufficiently different from Hinduism to sustain itself against the traditional faith. By modern times the Buddhists had so completely lost their position that most Indians did not even know there were any Buddhists in the country. Indeed, there were only a handful, scattered in out-of-the-way places — along the Himalayan range, in the hills of Bengal — plus a few priests here and there.

When I began to write this book, there were only 200,000 Buddhists in India; now there are nearly three million. This extraordinary increase dates from the twenty-five hundredth anniversary, in 1956, of the Parinirvana (Enlightenment) of Gautama the Buddha, which was celebrated with great pomp. (Indians are immensely proud of the fact that the Buddha was an Indian and Hindus do not reject him, although they do not worship him specially; as an avatar of Vishnu, he has a place in the Hindu pantheon.) This anniversay was the occasion for one of the largest mass religious conversions in history. More than half a million Harijans suddenly became Buddhists.

These conversions are understandable in the light of the personality of Dr. Ambedkar, the undisputed leader of the Harijans of Western India. Before Independence Dr. Ambedkar had opposed Gandhi's method of obtaining full citizenship for Harijans. Dr. Ambedkar wanted the British Government to grant them separate electorates, and Gandhi went on a hunger strike in protest against his plan. Gandhi won and, as a result, Dr. Ambedkar became increasingly bitter. As time went by, he felt more and more strongly that not enough was being done for the Harijans. The British gave him a chance to play a more important role when they nominated

him Law Minister. Dr. Ambedkar was the minister who
piloted the Indian Constitution and the Hindu Code Bill
through the Indian Parliament. After the Bill was finally
taken out of his hands, because, as he believed, of the Hindu
feeling that Hindu law could not be reformed by a Harijan,
Dr. Ambedkar decided to change his religion in the hope that
by ceasing to be Hindus the Harijans might become citizens
in fact as they are in law. So it was that 200,000 Harijans became Buddhists at the same time as their leader in protest
against caste oppression. An even larger conversion took place
three months later when Dr. Ambedkar died of a sudden
heart attack. At least 300,000 Harijans took the Buddhist
oath by the funeral pyre of their beloved leader. It remains to
be seen whether Dr. Ambedkar's shortcut to equality will work.
Conversions of this sort, without an adequate number of
religious teachers to back them up, do not always last.

THE PARSIS

The Parsis are the descendants of the people who escaped
into India by boat from Persia in the middle of the seventh
century when the Zoroastrians were defeated by the Moslems.
The Hindus welcomed them to their shores, and the Parsis
in turn adopted many Hindu customs, from dress and language
to food and certain domestic rituals. The adaptation was merely
formal, never fundamental, and this tiny community — perhaps originally only a couple of thousand refugees — remained
a little world of its own, accepted yet quite separate. Hindu indifference accounts for the fact that there are virtually
no instances of Parsi conversion to Hinduism.

Parsis are nonproselytizing monotheists; they regard fire as
God's most powerful symbol and pray to Him by facing the
sun or in a Fire Temple. They expose their dead to vultures in
Towers of Silence, because they do not want to pollute the
elements — earth, water, fire. Parsis believe, broadly speaking,
that there is a perpetual fight between the forces of Good and
Evil, and that it is their duty to side with the forces of Good.

This perhaps is why Parsis have such a striking record of personal and business integrity.

There are now 100,000 Parsis in India, and they are treated well. They have more than their numerical share of government jobs. Today indeed they have a great advantage over other communities because they are among India's most modern people. As there were none of the elaborate taboos of the Hindus and the Moslems in their religion, they took rapidly to new ways. Also, they are concentrated in India's most advanced industrial center, the city of Bombay, which their enterprise did so much to develop.

It may well be that modern India will develop on the Parsi pattern because while the equally modern Sikh is a rural or a martial type, the Parsi is the managerial type of which the new India is so short. The Parsis were the first Indians to live in blocks of apartments; now most city people, whatever their religion, live in apartments. The first Indian industrialists were Parsi; now they are largely Hindu and Jain. Even many of the first nationalists were Parsi. The whole of India is beginning to follow the trail blazed by this remarkable community.

THE JEWS

Like the Hindus and the Parsis, the Jews do not believe in conversion. For that reason they have managed to survive in India, despite their few numbers. There are perhaps 30,000 Jews in India, most of whom are Beni Israelis. The latter arrived and settled in India two thousand years ago — or so they claim. They are now physically indistinguishable from their Hindu neighbors because they intermarried with Hindus in the early days, although intermarriage is now forbidden. The Beni Israelis have taken on their neighbors' social customs but have retained the Jewish belief in the equality of man before man and God.

There is a peculiar Jewish enclave, the Jews of Cochin, who claim that their ancestors fled Jerusalem at the time of the second sacking of the Temple of King Solomon. The rulers of Cochin granted them land and full religious rights. These Jews of Cochin, now perhaps three thousand in all, never intermarried. Strange as it may seem, though, they adopted the Hindu caste system. They have three castes, one of which, if not actually untouchable, is at least prohibited from entering the temples of the top one hundred families.

After Independence and the creation of Israel, a number of Indian Jews left for Israel. The Beni Israelis settled there quietly and were not heard from again. The Jews of Cochin, on the other hand, came back with harrowing tales of how they were made to work: they said they were actually expected to use their hands!

Minorities are welcome and safe in India on one condition: they must not proselytize. No Hindu objects to a person's change of faith as the result of an inner conviction or the shining example of a better way, but he will not tolerate militant proselytizing. This is partly because the Hindu has had enough of being told that the Devil is black and partly because any genuinely nonmilitant faith finds proselytizing offensive and dangerous to its cherished values. The Indian attitude was well expressed by Gandhi when he was opposing the Arya Samaj, a revitalized militant Hindu sect: 'My Hindu instinct tells me that all religions are more or less true. All proceed from the same God, but all are imperfect because they have come down to us through imperfect human instrumentality. . . . No propaganda can be allowed which reviles other religions.' *

* *Young India*, 5 May 1924.

PART FOUR ❧ POLITICAL CHANGES

13

Gandhi

Gandhi was essentially an individualist and an experimenter. He was a man whose search for Truth was closely tied to an attempt to be good.

There is no such thing as 'Gandhism,' [he once said] and I do not want to leave any sect after me. I do not claim to have originated any new principle or doctrine. I have simply tried in my own way to apply the eternal truths to our daily life and problems. There is, therefore, no question of my leaving any code. . . . The opinions I have formed and the conclusions I have arrived at are not final. I may change them tomorrow. I have nothing new to teach the world. . . . All I have done is to try experiments in truth and non-violence on as vast a scale as I could.*

It is not easy to be good, and to the end, Gandhi fought a hard battle for the salvation of his individual soul: 'So long as a man does not of his own free will put himself last among his fellow creatures, there is no salvation for him. *Ahimsa* [nonviolence] is the farthest limit of humility. I know that I have still before me a difficult path to traverse.' †

Politics was part of his struggle to achieve truth:

For me the road to salvation lies through incessant toil in the service of my country and therethrough of humanity. I want to

---

* *Harijan*, 28 March 1936.
† Mahatma Gandhi, *My Experiments with Truth*, page 420.

identify myself with everything that lives. My national service is part of my training for freeing my soul from the bondage of flesh. Thus considered, my service may be regarded as purely selfish. I have no desire for the perishable kingdom of earth. I am striving for the Kingdom of Heaven. To see the universal and all-pervading Spirit of Truth face to face one must be able to love the meanest of creation as oneself. And a man who aspires after that cannot afford to keep out of any field of life. That is why my devotion to Truth has drawn me into the field of politics; and I can say without the slightest hesitation, and yet in all humility, that those who say that religion has nothing to do with politics do not know what religion means. My patriotism is for me a stage in my journey to the land of eternal freedom and peace. Thus it will be seen that for me there are no politics devoid of religion.*

To speak of Gandhism is to misunderstand — to refuse to understand — Gandhi. Only a particular spirit of compassion and equality as an active force can be called Gandhian. This is why the influence of Gandhi cannot be perceived in the new India in any but the broadest sense. Economically India is becoming modern and industrial; Gandhi's economics were old-fashioned and rural. As a result, his economics has been rejected as completely as his politics has been accepted.

When Gandhi died, Nehru mourned that 'the light has gone.' Indeed, Gandhi died with his task unfinished. Had he lived, India's economic progress might have been delayed, but India's social revolution would have gained momentum, for Gandhi had a unique gift for moving mountains. His approach was so practical as to be irresistible. For example, when he was asked if he believed in communication with spirits he answered:

I never receive communications from the spirits of the dead. I have no evidence warranting a disbelief in the possibility of such communications. But I do strongly disapprove of the practice of holding or attempting to hold such communications. They are often deceptive and are products of imagination. The practice is harmful both to the medium and the spirits, assuming the possi-

* *Young India*, 3 April 1924, and *My Experiments with Truth*, page 420.

bility of such communications. It attracts and ties to the earth
the spirit so invoked, . . . As for the medium, it is a matter of
positive knowledge with me that all those within my experience
have been deranged or weak-brained and disabled for practical
work whilst they were holding, or thought they were holding, such
communications. I can recall no friend of mine who having held
such communication had benefited in any way.*

Gandhi applied the same down-to-earth logic to the problems of the monkey scourge and India's worthless cattle.
And, because he spoke to Hindus as a Hindu in the name of
Hinduism, he was able to remold Hinduism as no five-year
plan can. He was the greatest reformer in Hindu history. The
reformation continues, slowly, irreversibly, but its course has
lost Gandhi's remorseless certainty.

Because he thought in such simple religious terms, he made
politics simple. He was a democrat and a nationalist because
he believed that it was bad for men's self-respect, for the
development of their souls, to be governed by others.
Whether government by others was or was not better for
them in any material sense was to him fundamentally irrelevant. For him it was simply wrong. Therefore, he had to bring
the people into politics, for it was their self-respect and
their development that concerned him. He was successful
because he alone was able to translate politics into the people's
terms. Gandhi made the ordinary villager the dominant
factor in Indian politics. He also taught the other Indian
classes to see India as a country whose heart was in its villages
and whose problems were to find food and clothing and
occupation for the inhabitants of the villages.

Gandhi's permanent contributions to India were fundamental. His belief in the equality of man and man was translated socially into the drive against untouchability and politically into adult suffrage. Adult suffrage meant for Gandhi
woman's suffrage. He was the greatest feminist of all: 'I am
uncompromising in the matter of woman's rights. In my

* Young India, 12 August 1929.

opinion she should labour under no legal disability not suffered by man. I should treat the daughters and the sons on a footing of perfect equality.' *

His belief that the end never justifies the means has had a profound effect on India's leaders. But for Gandhi's insistence on rightful means, these leaders might have been deflected from their democratic course in their despair at the difficulties of their task during the period of transition.

Perhaps even a greater contribution of Gandhi's to India has been the restoration of Indian self-respect. He was a little man who went about half naked, toothless, leaning on two young girls. Yet, by his very simplicity, he challenged the assumption of the British that material superiority was a sign of moral superiority. In their supreme arrogance the viceroys had inscribed in gold letters over the Delhi Secretariat: 'Liberty will not descend to a people. A people must raise themselves to liberty. It is a blessing that must be earned before it can be enjoyed.' Gandhi showed India how to earn her liberty without bitterness or rancor.

Gandhi was unique. A Saint through Action. The yogis and reformers who preceded him took little interest in social and political problems. They either sat on their mountain tops or in their hermitages or, like the Buddha, they preached to the masses. Gandhi, however, made no distinction between religion and politics. He did not distinguish between Caesar and God, because Caesar is merely an element of the divine universe. For him nothing existed apart from the universe. As he could not dissociate religion from life, or life from religion, Gandhi set himself actively to create conditions that might help to usher in the Kingdom of Earth. He was not concerned with economic notions or material equality. He was concerned with human equality — equality between black and white, Brahmin and Harijan, man and woman, rich and poor, ruler and ruled.

An Indian scholar told me that 'Gandhi was Britain's

* *Young India,* 17 October 1929.

parting gift to India.' It is true that Gandhi felt perfectly at home in Britain, so much so that he joined a 'No Breakfast' society in Manchester. He was influenced by the ideas he found in Ruskin and in an English translation of Tolstoy. He followed in the footsteps of British suffragettes and Irish national heroes. He fasted to achieve his demands. (He applied to Indian politics the weapon first invented by Deak Ferencz, the Hungarian nationalist whose passive non-co-operation with the Austrian Emperor peacefully won for Hungary its Constitution.) There is no doubt that Gandhi's fight for social equality was made easier because the British felt much as he did about untouchability, the plight of Hindu widows, and child marriages. In the field of social reform, there was no clash of interests, for the British administered India; they did not colonize it. Therefore, their status and their standards of living were not threatened by social equality. Only over the timing of independence was there room for conflict. Finally, British rule gave Gandhi not only a language, but also twentieth-century means of communication — from the railways to the telegraph and the newspapers — with which to reach his fellow countrymen directly, without distortions or delays.

To say, however, that Gandhi was Britain's parting gift to India is to overlook both the realities of the age in which he was born and the profound impact of his environment. Gandhi's mother was deeply religious. Rajkot, where he spent his adolescence, was steeped in the Jain tradition of nonviolence. And, finally, he was essentially a Hindu, a man of action who applied the Gita's commandment to every sphere of life: 'Your motive in working should be to set others, by your example, on the path of duty.'

14

Bhoodan and Gramdan

BHOODAN

Parallel to the organized land reforms and Community Projects, a one-man revolution is sweeping India's villages — the revolution of Bhoodan. This is the last flicker of the old way; its roots are in Hindu renunciation and in rural solidarity. Bhoodan is a Gandhian alternative to the Japanese or Chinese style of land reform; it is essentially Indian.

Bhoodan, which means 'the giving of land,' was started by Acharya Vinoba Bhave, who was Gandhi's ideal civil disobeyer; as such he spent many years in jail, although he is not interested in politics. He believes that land is an element like air and that every man has a right to a share of it. He believes also in love and nonviolence. He is opposed to money, in favor of barter, opposed to contraception and in favor of abstinence. He speaks eighteen languages, including French, Persian, Arabic, and Sanskrit. His favorite books are dictionaries because they show the oneness of mankind. He has an ulcer, dysentery, lumbago, and a nasty cough. In his photographs he resembles Rodin's John the Baptist, frail and imperfect, with an ascetic face and a Gothic beard.

In 1951 Vinoba Bhave was in Hyderabad, where the Communists held the district of Telengana by terror and the police fought them with counterterror. Telengana is very poor; there are a few big landlords and many landless people. Vinoba

Bhave went to villages where the Army feared to go; he talked
of love and nonviolence to peasants, landlords, and Communists. One day eighty landless laborers asked him for land.
Vinoba Bhave turned to the landed villagers: 'You heard your
brothers. They want land. I have no land. Give them land.'
It sounded so simple that one of them at once gave a hundred
acres. This was the beginning of Bhoodan. Since then, Vinoba
Bhave has been on the road, walking from village to village,
getting land for the poor. 'I come to loot you with love. I am
not begging. I ask for what is mine. If you give with love you
will stop Communism and hate.' From Hyderabad to Delhi,
from Delhi to the Uttar Pradesh, from the Uttar Pradesh to
Bihar, from Bihar to Kerala, he travels on foot. He will die —
soon, perhaps — but his work will remain.

People thought him mad when in April 1951 he announced
that he would get fifty million acres — one sixth of India's
cultivable land — for its ten million landless families. At first
he got little: five acres here, two acres there, bad land, land
under litigation. One man might give everything; another,
only a token. Vinoba Bhave takes all — good land and bad —
because he values the gift of the poor most — 'If the poor
give, the rich must give.' In six years he has received over four
and a half million acres from over half a million donors. He
has already distributed over 400,000 acres. The State Governments have had to enact legislation to accelerate the transfer
of land. Once the owner, in front of two witnesses, signs the
printed form giving the survey number of his land gift, his
land is the property of Vinoba Bhave. In the one case where
a donor changed his mind, the form was returned to him.
Not all the given land is cultivable; some has to be reclaimed
or freed from litigation; some is fit only for grazing or for
forest. The land is distributed according to an invariable
routine. The villagers meet to determine who needs land
most. There is nearly always agreement, but if there is not
enough land — each family gets five acres — lots are drawn.
The land is given to a family in trusteeship, for no Bhoodan

land can be sold, mortgaged, rented, or left fallow. If it is not used it lapses back into the pool of land to be distributed. Sometimes there are delays in distribution, but these are technical and administrative.

From Bhoodan ('gift of land') Vinoba Bhave has gone on to Sampattidan ('gift of wealth'), in which the donor gives one sixteenth of his income to newly settled land holders for the purchase of bullocks, seeds, and tools. Each of the workers of a cotton mill donated a day's wages — which added up to four thousand dollars — and, because the workers gave, the managers had to give. There are also Kuadan, the giving once of one hundred dollars, which is the cost of a well; Shramdan, the gift of voluntary labor; and Jivandan, the gift of one's life — that is, its dedication forever to Bhoodan work. Vinoba Bhave has gathered over six hundred and fifty lives, including that of Mr. Jayaprakash Narayan, India's leading Socialist. Formerly leader of the Praja Socialist Party, Narayan retired from politics to devote himself to Bhave's cause. After Prime Minister Nehru, he is probably the only Indian leader who has more than regional appeal.

Bhoodan is a controversial cure for India's ills and the tensions of the atomic age. On the debit side there are the inefficiency of its administration by amateurs, the poverty of much of the land that is given, and the fact that Bhoodan is a one-man show. This means that while Vinoba Bhave can get thousands of acres of land with ease, Jayaprakash Narayan can get only a couple of hundred acres with difficulty. On the credit side, there are: the very existence of Narayan, which assures continuity of leadership; the role of the Government which, for example, enters the changes of ownership in the Record of Rights; the fact that, even if only a third of the land donated is good, it is still a great deal and much of the remaining land will eventually be reclaimed; the thousands of families who are now settled on land, which adds to political stability; and the orientation that has been given to the constructive activities of Gandhi's followers who felt lost after Independence.

To understand Bhoodan one must see it an action. That is why I traveled with Vinoba Bhave for a few days. First, I went to the Bhoodan office in Gaya, where the Buddha first saw the Light. Gaya is in Central Bihar, which is a province north-west of Bengal and due south of Nepal. Central Bihar is one of the hottest places in Asia. In summer, the average daily temperature is 117° F. in the shade, and every day a nagging dust storm called 'Loo' rages from ten in the morning to five in the afternoon, causing gritty teeth, burning eyes, and a fever, also called 'Loo.' The Bhoodan office is in the tumble-down court-yard of the station's 'pilgrim's halt.' There gifts are tabulated and registered by workers who drink cool water from earthen jars and who sweat profusely. Everybody sweats. They pour water on their heads and clothes and wrap wet towels around themselves; everybody drips and drips and drips. One worker, Devi Ben was suffering from 'Loo' fever; she lay on the floor semi-conscious yet cheerful. In her native Madras such heat is unknown; she suffered more than I did.

Hari Singh told me of his bitterness toward the Congress Party as 'the real murderer of Gandhi: Gandhi was a prin-ciple, a way of life. The Congress program is the negation of that way of life. I went with Vinoba Bhave to Telengana. We could not believe our eyes. Our own government, a Con-gress government, was as ruthless as the Communists. In-deed, at times, the Communists were more humanitarian; they distributed land. Vinoba Bhave would have gone Com-munist if not for his deep-rooted belief in love and nonvio-lence. Congress has kept the old bottles with Gandhian tags but there is nothing Gandhian left inside.'

At dawn Hari Singh and I boarded the train, which inched along the eighty miles toward the village where Bhave was to be that night. The train stopped eventually at a crossing, where we transferred to an *ekka* (a horse cart hanging from two wheels). By the time we arrived, my bones were thoroughly ground together from hopping over ruts, diving into river beds, and cutting across paddy fields. Gandhi's granddaughter, Sumitra, greeted us — energetic, cheerful, a chic tomboy, amusing like her grandfather, vital like her grandmother, not weighed down by her illustrious heritage. She said of Gandhi: 'He always thought me headstrong. He accepted me. He loved me without wanting to reform me.'

The village honored its guests with a feast. There were gallons of 'Loo' (sour mango squash and salt) to drink. The outer courtyard was swept at once with a broom of twigs, then sprinkled with water and smeared with cow-dung paste. The pungent, disinfectant smell of dung floated above the dust from the coat of mud that was our tablecloth. In a corner four huge earthenware cauldrons simmered over open-hearth fires which smoked like small chimneys. Landless laborers churned the contents, their sweat dripping into the brew. Leaves were spread out like mats for us to squat upon. More leaves were placed in front of us for plates. One of the men splashed a dollop of rice on each leaf. That was followed by dhal (pulse), which trickled onto our leaves from cupped hands innocent of soap but familiar with sweat and earth. Pickled mango slices, curried ladyfingers, curried potatoes, and fried eggplant were stacked in little mounds by the huge mountain of rice. At the end of the meal, curds were brought around in dirty cupped hands; there my personal fastidiousness got the better of my new valor and I could not eat it. I could hope that hot food was germicidal, but not cold curds. This was our meal, the result of the combined efforts of the entire village.

Sumitra whispered, 'I do not like this. They should serve us with a spoon. Biharis *are* dirty. But we must eat or else they will feel hurt. They have done their best for us.' It was best to forget the hands that served us, the flies attracted by the smell of food, the near-by cows, and the village garbage dump only a stone's throw across the courtyard. Brahm

Prakash cheered me up: 'How well planned, indeed, how labor-saving. Just think of it. When you finish eating there is no need to get up to throw away the plate; you can toss it into the rubbish heap.' It was so clear that the village had done us as proud as it could. The men hung over us so anxiously, refilling our leaves, that it would have been heartless to be fussy.

Eating rice and dhal with one's fingers is not easy when the plate is waist-high at a table. When the plate is level with one's crossed knees, it becomes quite an art. So is drinking without touching the glass with one's lips — there is only one glass for all to share. Indian villagers watching an outsider struggle with clumsy fingers, dribbling dhal and splashing himself with water, are as delighted as children watching a game. They towered over me in friendly approval at my efforts, and Sumitra encouraged me with her deft example. She can actually drink a whole glass of water from a distance, without interrupting herself once to swallow air or tilt the glass back to stop the flow.

Strangely enough, although the village was treating us like kings, we were served by Harijans. This is the natural outcome of the strict purdah system practiced in Shahabad District. The women cannot come out and caste men will not cook for us, since in this part of Bihar cooking is a female occupation. So the task was given to landless laborers. Sumitra fretted over this custom, the filth of the service, and the odd site of the meal — in the backyard by the rubbish dump. 'It is only because of "Baba" [Bhave] that we have to eat like this. "Bapu" [Gandhi] was most particular about hygiene. He always insisted that we cook our own food, and he was almost a maniac about organization; but "Baba" does not care about people and organization.' Indeed, Acharya Vinoba Bhave is concerned only with collecting land.

I met a few more of Bhave's disciples. Near by on the mud floor lay Gopi Sen, a giant of a man from Uttar Pradesh whose admirable body had been broken by the tormenting dust of 'Loo.' Having given his land to 'Baba,' he has given his life also. He lay there helpless, but his classical features were lighted by a smile that even fever could not sour. Sumitra wet his brow and I gave him mint drops. There was Santa, a dark, silent girl from Maharashtra. She ate but once a day, fasted twice a week, and seemed completely happy. And Vishnu, soft but determined, typed for Baba for one hundred dollars a year and gave one sixteenth of his income to Bhoodan. Tia, a child widow, shadowed the master like a Biblical figure, preparing his food, washing his feet, and playing the *zitar* for him in the blazing noon. Everyone was even-tempered; everyone suffered from the heat. It was so hot that two birds nesting over the thatch panted like dogs, with their beaks open and their tongues out.

At six in the evening, Vinoba Bhave came out for the prayer meeting. Never before in my years in India had a meeting been so silent. Perhaps two hundred villagers squatted in the small courtyard. Not a baby whined, not a dog barked. After prayers Vinoba Bhave spoke of the evil of violence and the blessing of love. 'If you tell me you cannot give land because you already have seven sons and only a small holding of land, I will answer: "I am your eighth son and I have come to take my rightful share." ' In the spreading shadows, lit only by a petrol lamp, I watched the faces pitted with small-pox, intent under wet towels and bulky turbans. At the end of Bhave's talk, fourteen donors gave him thirty-two hundred acres of land.

Then Vinoba Bhave had a cupful of curds, talked with Sumitra, and went to sleep. We dragged our aching bones to our sleeping place. Before I went to sleep, I overheard this discussion:

'What is your Bhoodan? All men are not equal. This is against nature,' argued the sub-inspector of police, a handsome swashbuckling man with a flaring mustache.

Gopi Sen replied, 'We must try. Bhoodan is what we make it. I am only a peasant, but "Baba" knows.' The moon rose

over the hilltops and dusted the scorched earth with silver,
while the guard and the disciple argued as if they were in
Galilee.

The next day began at three in the morning. We walked
nine miles before sunrise. Vinoba Bhave, slimmer and older
in the dangling light of the oil lamp, seemed hardly to touch
the earth as he led the way. 'Time is on my side; therefore,
I cannot lose,' he said about his race with illness. The gray
dust of Bihar stuck to his brown ankles as if the earth itself
moved with him. Sixteen to twenty miles a day is his average
but as he was unwell, we went only nine miles. After five
miles I gave in. I lay on the edge of a well watching ants and
listening to the water trickle. I was sorry when a rattle-trap
jeep arrived to pick me up. There had been so much peace
everywhere, within and without — peace that must have ema-
nated from Vinoba Bhave, so complete that nothing mattered
but the knowledge that it existed. My mind stood before me,
bared of its vulgarities, motives, make-believes, stripped naked
by truth. The chief Minister of Bombay once said that he had
experienced 'absolute peace and the total absence of desire'
in the presence of a very holy man. So it is in the presence of
Vinoba Bhave.

He acts as a catalyst; he denies himself, yet he is always the
cause of action. That evening a landlord bared his conscience
in front of Vinoba Bhave's bed: 'I am a poor man. I have
already given two hundred and fifty acres of land. I have many
sons and they have many children. How can I give more? I
would like to give, but I must think of them. What must I
do?' Vinoba Bhave is asleep — a small clump of brown on a
white sheet, hardly bigger than my little boy.

Since the time Vinoba Bhave was beaten up by priests for
taking Harijans into a temple he has been slightly deaf, so
my questions had to be written. Of my seventeen questions,
only one matters: 'Why is it that I have no desire to speak
with you, or stay with you, yet that I feel at peace and have
no curiosity left? Does it make sense?' This is his answer:

'Talking is the least part of things. We feel. We love. We meditate. Talking should be used to fraternize. Your question is not senseless. Silence is better than speech. It works wonders.'

The third day I hovered around him for hours. In a meeting of workers, a landlord who had already given two thousand acres the year before announced that he would give another two thousand and keep only thirty acres for himself and his family. In a public meeting Bhave thundered: 'God will ask you: Did "Baba" come to your village? Did he tell you to give freedom to your wives? Have you done so? I came twenty months ago and your women are still in jail.' (There is strict purdah in these parts of Bihar.) Then he announced that he had received 4,820 acres — not counting the landlord's two thousand — from thirty-seven donors. All through the day he refused himself to me. He does not get involved with individuals. As he told the prayer meeting: 'We must all solve our problems ourselves.'

The fourth day the heat was unbearable. After lunch Santa wept softly. I swallowed a bottle of salt tablets, Vishnu could not type, and Sumitra cried in her sleep. My torch fell out of my pocket, burning. I thought it was a short circuit, but it was the heat concentrated in the metal casing. Vinoba Bhave seemed beyond the world, quiet, cool. He dictated to Tia the whole afternoon, yet in the morning he had run for nine miles and crossed a river, waist-deep in water, while we followed in canoes. The last mile to the village he was far ahead of us, followed by small children flying homemade flags and singing songs — formidable crusaders of love, an old man and children getting land for the poor.

Could Vinoba Bhave be effective outside India? The answer is yes. That he is a scholar, dark skinned, Gandhian, is irrelevant. Vinoba Bhave is a saint, and saints are universal. If one day he came to London or New York, half naked, barefoot, quiet, asking for a room in your house for the poor, you would give it — gladly or grumblingly — but you would give it, just as the landlords of Bihar do, for Vinoba Bhave is irresistible.

As time passes and as my impressions blur, I am no longer so sure that Bhoodan is required to solve India's land problem; but, frankly, I do not care. To me, Bhoodan has been an experience so unique that it is impossible to be impartial about it. Whether Bhoodan succeeds, whether Vinoba Bhave achieves his target, is immaterial. What matters to me is the discovery that in detachment there is peace. Yet I feel no special gratitude to Vinoba Bhave for this discovery. One is not grateful to the sun for making it possible to see. Vinoba Bhave's presence is not required to maintain the kind of light he creates; for his is the light within, the light of knowledge which nothing can destroy.

Gandhi? Bhave? They are as different as the poles. Gandhi, human, lively, pragmatic, full of mischief, wanting to be loved, tyrannical yet considerate, admirable organizer, madly fiddling with details, demanding the surrender of self from his disciples, compromising with his supporters. Bhave, inhuman, dogmatic, always serious, detached, indifferent, a poor organizer, demanding nothing that is not offered. Gandhi, red flame, strong and warm. Bhave, white flame, unreal and cool.

GRAMDAN

The Bhoodan experiment was threatening to become a failure. Two years had passed and yet much of the donated land had not been distributed. Suddenly a miracle took place.

Acharya Vinoba Bhave was walking through the blue hills of Orissa, a province bordering the Bay of Bengal, southwest of Calcutta. He was asking for land for some of India's poorest aboriginals, the Khonds. The Khonds responded to his appeal not by giving him land but by giving him the whole of their villages. Acharya Vinoba Bhave reacted to the gift in a way typical of his approach: he simply marched on asking for more land. But, before he abandoned the Khonds to their new fate, he called in Annasaheb Sahasrabuddhe. And so began Gramdan — the gift of villages.

Of all the Gandhians I have met, none is more impressive, in his own way, than Annasaheb. Tough, rugged, practical, and ruthless, he is a great organizer and a great realist who does not confuse means with ends. Most impressive of all, he never underrates a difficulty. Talking to Annasaheb, one cannot but admire the foresight of Gandhi, who trained men to serve each of India's needs — a political heir, Nehru; a moral heir, Jayaprakash Narayan (the Socialist leader who is now Bhave's follower); a spiritual heir, Acharya Vinoba Bhave; and a practical heir, Annasaheb. Recognizing Annasaheb's genius for organization and the intensity of his desire to do constructive rather than political work, Gandhi entrusted him with the world's largest co-operative — the All-India Spinners Association, with more than two million members and branches all over the subcontinent. In the days of the struggle for freedom, the purpose of the association was to spin and market yarn to replace British goods, and also to build up a sense of nationalism and a core of disciplined and selfless workers. After Independence, Annasaheb began to wonder whether spinning was enough by itself. What seemed to be needed was a means to awaken the villagers and to help them fight poverty. He found in Gramdan the answer to his quest.

Gramdan is a revolution so unique that it is difficult to convey all its implications — a revolution which, by the end of 1956, was being carried out quietly, unnoticed, by 200,000 aboriginals in Koraput.

Koraput is a district, backward even in backward Orissa, where everything is blue — from the tall blue hills infested with wild beasts to the rich paddy fields of blue valleys dotted with blue lakes. It is one of India's major rice exporting districts, but its people are among India's poorest. The average income for a family of five is only about thirty-five dollars per year, because the crops are grabbed by money-lenders, who have a complete stranglehold over the Khonds. While trainloads of rice go chugging out of the stations, the villagers feed on roots and leaves for eight months in the year. They are so honest that it would not enter their heads to refuse to surrender their crop in payment for a debt they have already paid back ten times over in their ignorance, and they are so innocent that they do not even realize they are being cheated. The Khonds are a gay people who believe in magic and free love, and who feed their hunger with drums, songs, and country brew. They shift-cultivate and believe that 'land belongs to nobody's grandfather.' Their villages are small and delightfully painted, homogeneous — everybody in them is a Khond — and compact. At Gobarpalli, for example, there is only one street. On either side, houses and verandas line up, resembling tiny pigeon holes under one long, very low roof, and the animals huddle together at the end of the street in the corral, which is fortified with thorns against tigers. At Kumbhar Peta, the potter's village, the houses are separate from each other and scattered, but the firing kiln is common. Not all Khond villages share a roof or a fire, but at festival time, the men go roaming everywhere over their blue hills, singing and dancing from village to village. Blue-painted, peacock-feathered, they wander for weeks, fed by villagers on the way. Such poverty and unity led easily to the step of pooling their lands and forming Gramdans.

In a Gramdan the land is owned by the village, the villager is a mere trustee. When I visited Koraput, two and a half years after Acharya Vinoba Bhave's passage, there were already more than 1300 Gramdans. One seventh of the land and one sixth of the population of the district were involved in this extraordinary revolution. Gramdan spreads like an oilstain, one hundred and fifty Hindu (as distinct from casteless) villages have followed the example of their tribal neighbors, and the Government of Orissa has amended the law to meet Gramdan needs.

How does Gramdan work? After the villagers donate their land, the Council decides how many acres each villager is to keep. This depends on the size of his family, his status and, if he was a landowner before, on the inducement required to make him co-operate. Holdings are to be periodically reviewed by the Council according to performance and need. In a few villages it has been decided to put some land to collective use. But on the whole the villagers decided that they wanted to cultivate their land on the principle of private trusteeship rather than in any co-operative or collective way. The really remarkable feature of Gramdan is that everything is decided by the villagers themselves, after discussion, in the most democratic of fashions.

However, if Gramdan was not to be merely a new means of distributing poverty, outside help had to be provided. Skilled men and money were needed. Annasaheb called up old Gandhian workers who had retired to the rarefied atmosphere of their ashrams (institutionalized retreats). Today their old routine has been broken, for the ashrams are closed and the workers are active once more fighting poverty. Money, too, has been found in various places — the All-India Spinners Association, the Central Government's Department for Tribal Welfare, the Reserve Bank, and donations to Acharya Vinoba Bhave.

Before he started organizing, Annasaheb knew that selfless dedication could only carry the movement just so far. It needed to attract people who could help organize and advance the cause. He reasoned that if Gramdan offered the older generation, such as the Gandhian workers, scope for action, how much more would it appeal to the younger generation! Annasaheb knew that India is full of intellectuals who are still sufficiently impetuous to believe that individuals can change society but who are disillusioned by the cruelties of Communism and the bureaucracy and red tape of Socialism. All he had to do was to make them aware of Gramdan.

Annasaheb's method is simplicity itself: he invites students and administrators to visit Koraput. The sight of the villages usually produces the effect Annasaheb desires, for more and more of these young people come to stay and work. At Limbaguda, Mr. Parekh, the son of a millionaire and an Oxford graduate, lives humbly, like a villager, and tries, by his example and advice, to help his neighbors. At Bandikhar, Mr. Patel, an engineer, directs land reclamation work and runs a residential institute, where he trains local schoolboys to become surveyors. Mr. Patel has cut his own pay from fifty dollars to fifteen dollars a month; his students, who are paid while in training, get half as much. At Burja, Mr. Apte runs a residential Agricultural School for Village Level Workers. After nine months training they are given half as much pay as they would get in a Government Community Project. And, at the top, there is Mr. Datye, from the Central Water and Power Commission, on long-term leave from his Government job. Datye is as proud of his villagers as of his three children. His lovely wife does not mind living on less than half her husband's old pay. She is so enthused by events around her that she does not care. With sparkling eyes, Datye and his wife explain: 'Do you realize that all the canals, all the dams, all the contours, all the schemes the villagers put up, have proved sound! And in months and months of surveying, it has been impossible for us to suggest a single scheme they had not already listed! And people say that villagers are stupid! Villagers are not stupid. They are far wiser than we are. The only thing they require is technical guidance.'

Over half the twenty-nine million dollars budgeted for projects for the next five years is for land improvement. Once the villagers have agreed on a project, they next decide how many free labor days each family must contribute. A family never contributes more than five free days a month because 'the poor cannot afford to be charitable, even to themselves, for they must eat.' The remaining days are paid for at prevailing rates, and if the villagers are busy they hire outsiders.

'We must never forget to fit our schemes into the villager's life. For example, during the day he needs his children to mind goats and babies. The fact that he cannot send them to school does not mean that he does not value education,' says

Mr. Parekh, who is going to start residential night schools, where the children will also be taught hygiene, and games and gardening. To such schools parents will gladly send their children.

Enthusiasm does not blind the organizers to their difficulties. The moment a village becomes a Gramdan, the land can no longer be pledged against loans, and the villager, who has no economic staying power, must therefore be helped from outside. He does not own his bullocks, but he needs bullocks to grow food. With the money-lender out of the picture, money has to come from the organization. Already more than a thousand pairs of bullocks have been distributed in two hundred villages. But that is not enough. Gramdan is not an end, it is a means to fighting poverty and ignorance. An immense responsibility lies with the organization. That is why Annasaheb has decided to concentrate on seven blocks — 427 villages in all. The rest, he has declared, are the responsibility of the Government and the people. But the rest cannot wait for the Government to take action in due course; they must be helped at once. The result is that Annasaheb has had to obtain action from the Reserve Bank which will automatically underwrite credit for every Gramdan.

Besides getting credit, Annasaheb is trying to make the villagers self-sufficient and market-conscious through co-operatives. When no one can read or write, it is difficult to run a co-operative. Annasaheb has too much wisdom and experience to believe, as so many of the less-experienced politicians do, that co-operation is easy or that it should be forced on the villagers from above. What he has done is to form an Apex Society, run by experienced co-operators, with affiliate branches in each group of villages under the control of the villagers themselves. It does not matter how they do their accounts — such as figuring with twigs or the other rough-and-ready methods to which they are accustomed. In time they will become sufficiently familiar with the operation of a co-operative and sufficiently educated to be able to participate at the Apex also. The Apex co-operative buys up all the produce of the villages, and the branches sell back to the villagers consumer goods. The merchant and the money-lender have been eliminated.

It is too soon to say whether this great experiment will succeed. But if it does, it will achieve many great things. It will give the Parekhs, the Datyes, and the Patels a *raison d'être.* It will provide the Government with a valuable guide for its own development programs. It will lift the people of Koraput out of their terrible poverty. And it will do all this without any break from the past, in harmony with the tradition of the Gita, the ancient village organization, and Mahatma Gandhi.

15

Community Projects

If India is to progress, her 558,089 villages must change their traditional way of life, in which agriculture is an age-old art and the Indian villager its skilled practitioner. As agriculture in general has become more scientific, the Government has been pondering means of introducing these modern techniques to the Indian peasant. The way has been pointed out by an American who had nothing to do with agriculture. His name is Albert Mayer.

India owes more to Albert Mayer than perhaps to any other single foreigner; yet his name is known to few, and even those few are beginning to forget. A prosperous architect, Albert Mayer is essentially a product of American urbanism and modern technology. Most men have a latent urge to be useful, to do good. Few are equipped to respond to that urge. They may have the know-how, but, unless they are missionaries, they may have neither the time nor the money. Or, if they have money, they may still lack opportunity. Albert Mayer had everything: know-how, money, opportunity. It was the accident of World War II that took him out of the comfort of his house in New York City to build airfields in the swamps of Bengal. He made many Indian friends. One day he met Nehru, who had just been released from a British jail. The two men liked each other instantly. Mayer said that although India was fifty years behind the West, India could catapult through time; there was no need to repeat experiments the West had made years before. India could benefit from Western experience. Mayer suggested that one way India might advance was to build model villages. Six months later, Nehru wrote to ask whether Mayer would care to undertake such a project when India was free. Mayer accepted. In the spring of 1946, Nehru, who had become the head of the Interim Government of undivided India, asked Mayer to come back.

Albert Mayer spent a lot of time prospecting for the site of the ideal Indian village. Finally, he settled for the small village of Maheva in the district of Etawah, a night's journey east of the capital at Delhi. From Mayer's point of view, Maheva had five advantages. The Chief Minister of Uttar Pradesh was eager for the project to begin in his State, and his support was valuable. Maheva had a small temple with a courtyard of tiny rooms; this solved the problem of housing while the village was being constructed. The area was neither rich nor poor. It was neither too near nor too far from a town. Its soil was eroding.

For two years, Mayer spent many summer nights in a little room off the temple yard, living simply, drawing his own water from the well, mixing with the villagers, talking to local officials, training a team of dedicated men. To his surprise, he discovered that the villagers did not want an ideal village: they were too poor and could not believe in a better future, for the present was already so much worse than the past. So Albert Mayer, who had come to India to build an ideal village, started a project to raise the standard of living of the villagers, so that one day they might want to live in an ideal village.

The village of Maheva became the center of the Etawah Pilot Project. By the end of 1948, the Etawah Project was strengthened by a handful of American and Indian experts selected by Albert Mayer. The Project expanded until it included three hundred villages. Then it split in two; part of the trained staff was sent to start a sister project at Gorakhpur, near the Nepal border, where conditions were quite different from Etawah. By that time, the First Five-Year Plan, partly as a result of the prodding of United States Ambassador Bowles, had incorporated the Etawah Pilot Project, made it India's, multiplied it, extended it, diluted it, and sprinkled India with as many such projects as possible.

Not only did Mayer's experiment give the Government of India the technique it was groping for, but it gave the United States Government and the Ford Foundation the ideal channel through which to help India effectively. The United States Government set up an agency called the Technical Co-operation Mission, which, by the end of 1956, had spent fourteen million dollars on equipment to help various parts of the Community Project Program. So far, the Ford Foundation has spent over eight million dollars on training personnel and lending experts. The contribution of the Ford Foundation has been useful out of all proportion to its size, because it has helped to fill gaps that might otherwise have developed into gulfs. It has all along been the silent partner of the Indian Government. The Indian Government could not have trained soon enough the personnel it needed had it not been for the experts and the training courses set up with the Foundation's assistance. The Projects were at all times run by the Government of India, which, together with the State governments, decided on the schemes and paid for most of the expenses of every kind and for all the personnel actually employed in the villages.

The Etawah Pilot Project was new not in its aims but in its method. Before the Projects, men like Brayne in Gurgaon, Captain Mohite in Bombay, and Sir Malcolm Darling in the Punjab had tried to make Indian villages more livable, Indian agriculture more efficient, and the people more educated. Brayne had supplied better seeds; Sir Malcolm established admirable co-operatives; Captain Mohite built schools by the score. In each case, the results depended entirely on the personality of the man who provided the inspiration. In each case, the inspiration flagged when he left.

At Etawah, on the other hand, men come and go, but the inspiration remains. Etawah maintains its continuity by continuous recruitment. At the same time, it offers full scope for individuality within the general framework of its programs, which are made more effective through concentration of personnel. There are 25 per cent more government servants now than there used to be, and all those who deal with the villagers have been trained in rural psychology and in the objectives and methods of the Project. Work began slowly at Etawah, at the villagers' and not at an administrator's pace. Etawah is a test tube in the open air, where action and reaction are studied until the best approach is evolved. The purpose of going slowly is to avoid mistakes which could bring about costly resistance from the villagers at a later stage.

Wherever villagers are convinced of the advantages of change, it has come swiftly and easily. But the advantages have to be obvious. At Etawah, adult education for men is very successful. The villager wants to read so that he does not get cheated, so that he can read the instructions on the wrappers of the insecticides he is being trained to use, and so that he can write postcards to his cousin in a distant town. He also wants to read the fortnightly adult education magazine *Mandir Se* (named after Albert Mayer's headquarters 'From the Temple'). It costs sixty cents a year and its paid circulation is forty thousand. It is the best Indian Government publication I have seen. One page is devoted to current news, one to local news, one to tips on animal husbandry, and one to seasonal crop information. It also gives crop prices. The back page, which is in very bold type, acts as a follow-up to the lessons; it has a little story, which is often religious.

Villagers willingly contribute a veranda for the adult education classes; the Panchayat pays for the kerosene, the chalk, the slates, and the fifteen rupees per month salary for the teacher. The teacher is a villager who can read and write and has had twenty-five days of training in adult education. He is not the regular schoolteacher, who is too blasé, too set in his ways, too tired in the evening, and too keen to cultivate his own field in his spare time. He is also not an urban student, who is too remote from village life. Lessons last one hour; then come games, music, drums, singing, and fun — that inimitable fun of the poor peasant who gets intoxicated by the rhythm of the drums and his own excitement.

The results of adult education were remarkable in the various schools I visited. In three months, pupils could read and write. I watched Ram Singh in a school, where perhaps twenty-five men had gathered after a day's work in the field, under the shadow of a kerosene lamp. Like Ram, they had come to learn to read and write. Ram's face was tense. His pink tongue studiously followed his calloused fingers in their delicate tracery on the slate: 'When my child is ill with small-pox I take him to the doctor for vaccination.' The sweat of concentration oozed from his forehead. He chanted the same sentence with the whole class. With the pride of a child, he showed me his slate, with its neat Devanagri (Hindi script) characters 'Ma, La, Ro.' 'Next time I sign a promissory note,' he told me proudly, 'I will be able to read it and know how much I have to pay.'

Just as villagers have taken to adult education, so they have taken to better agricultural techniques. The heart of agriculture, in India at least, is water. Already about ten tube wells had been sunk. One third of the money for them is contributed by the villages, one third comes from Government grants, and the rest is a Government loan. Next to water, the greatest need is for improved seeds. It took the Project three years to go from demonstration to saturation with improved wheat seeds, which were distributed by the Project's co-operative; they were to be paid for in seeds plus 25 per cent of the crop after the harvest. Improvement met with response in exact proportion to benefit. Improved farm tools are also popular. The traditional Indian plow is a forked branch of a tree, pointed at one end; it is light and cheap, but it is not very effective. At Etawah they added a sort of iron spear with a curve that turns the soil over as it plows. Indian sickles are made of heavy metal and are fairly blunt; at Etawah they are made with teeth, like a saw. Simple seed drills and dibblers are available to the villagers, who hitherto sowed, as in Victor Hugo's poem, with 'a wide and august sweep.' These tools save the villagers one third of their seeds.

This agricultural renaissance has made the area more prosperous. First, the villagers bought better bullocks. Next, they ate more and better food. Then they bought cloth and perhaps a kerosene lamp. Finally, they began to repair their houses or to build new ones. The Project introduced co-operative brickkilns, which have been enthusiastically received. If he has any extra money, the villager may buy a bicycle. Prosperity has so blossomed at Etawah that the money-lender has turned shopkeeper and daily wages have doubled in three years. One villager proudly explained that, with the thousand dollars his fifty acres now bring in every year, he could send his son to study medicine in England.

Etawah's techniques are being carried out all over India in modified forms. Below the picturesque Sahyadri Mountains are the hundred-odd villages of the Baglan Project. This Project, smaller than most, is typical of much that succeeds and fails. Villagers are always keen to improve their crops, but no individual will take the initiative. 'I would like to try a new groundnut seed, but nobody in my village has tried it yet. I must wait for someone to be the first,' explained one villager.

Change, to be accepted, has to be collective. That is why the Project runs demonstration plots on villagers' land, so that all can see for themselves what can be done just by using better seeds. The initial response has come from men like Raghunath Patil, who borrowed from the Project half the money for his five-hundred-dollar pump, and then, after seeing one demonstration plot sowed Cambodia cotton and improved millet on his fifteen-acre farm. Once the more prosperous Raghunath has made good, the smaller farmers will follow. Naturally this procedure has drawn much criticism that the Community Projects benefit the rich and, by contrast, make the poor poorer. This situation is inevitable: the rich are always in the forefront when it comes to doing better. But in due course, the poor too become less poor: they get more work and their children benefit from the new school even more than the children of the rich.

Next to agriculture, education for the young is the greatest success at Baglan. Many schools have been built with the co-operation of both the village and the Government, and more are being built. Children are not only taught to read and write; they are taught a trade as well. Adult education, however, has failed at Baglan. The adults are shy of learning from their children's teachers and they feel they are too tired to learn after a hard day in the field. The example of Etawah, where education is coated with the sugar of fun, has been lost on its way to Baglan.

When tangible results are not immediately apparent, the villagers have to be humored. Thus a nutrition expert persuaded some villagers not to throw away the water in which vegetables had been cooked: 'There was a bad mother-in-law who used to feed her son lots of rice but gave his wife only the rice water. The son grew thin and weak, the daughter-in-law strong and fat. "How can that be?" wondered the old woman, until a neighbor told her that all the goodness of the rice had gone into the water. The same is true of vegetables. Do not throw away the water in which you cook rice and vegetables.'

The Projects have been very successful in their campaign against malaria. It is popular to spray houses with D.D.T.; indeed, villagers demand a spraying if one is overdue. The incidence of malaria has already fallen from 50 per cent to 3 per cent in one year. Radios are in great demand; their cost is shared equally by the Government and the village, but the Government cannot afford to give a radio subsidy to more than a ratio of one set for every thousand villagers.

Village organization can speed up Project work. If one leader does something, the others do it, too. But village hierarchy can also be a great handicap. At Khubkera, where everyone agreed in principle that irrigation was a good thing, the building of a small dam was held up because the richer villagers, who valued their position more than anything else, refused to contribute their share and intimidated their neighbors into doing the same. They knew that if water became plentiful, equality would follow and they would lose some of their importance.

'I have paid at least twenty-five visits to Khubkera,' said the Project officer. 'They all say, "Yes, we will give the money." Yet no money comes. But we cannot use Government pressure, because that would be against the object of the scheme, which is to develop local leadership, not to increase local factions. I have tried to push the villagers into building roads they did not feel the need for. They all promised they would come. Somehow things kept going wrong. Carts had a way of not turning up when they were needed, and, if the carts were there, the people were not. When both people and equipment were on the site, local village strife got the upper hand. Finally I had to give up. I had killed myself going to the village, I had evoked no response — but I had learned a lesson. It is better to go slowly at the beginning. Once all agree they want the dam, the dam will be built in no time. For it is always easier to get people to do what they want to do.'

The greatest Indian revolution of all is expressed in this last sentence: 'It is always easier to get people to do what they want to do.' The people are the Government, and the Government is merely selling them new ideas and techniques. Indeed, the people of India and the Government are partners in making the new India. This new approach is more subtle and difficult than the old, where the Government gave orders which the people were expected to obey.

What is most important is that the Government official

must not look upon rural development as a sideline to the routine of collecting revenue and keeping order. Rural development must become a full-time endeavor, where ordering is replaced by 'showing' — by what Albert Mayer called the 'dirty hands method.' For the people and the Government to be true partners, they must work, hand in hand, side by side, without any barriers of prestige between officers and cultivators. Both must handle the spade, which means that the officers, conditioned by generations of caste, must feel that they are pioneers who are creating the new India; they must take up the work with enthusiasm. Enthusiasm must, however, be tempered with reality. The officers must refrain from forcing the village to meet targets laid down on paper miles away in the city; the targets must be ones the village itself thinks it can accomplish. For successful co-operation the officers must win and retain the confidence of their partners in development. They must never let them down. If they have announced a visit to the village, they must come on the appointed day, not a week later. If the villager goes to them for advice or a loan, they must be available. From having been almighty, they must become the traveling salesmen of the Government.

This is a lot to ask of an administration steeped in the tradition of its own importance. Yet the success of the rural revolution depends on the change of heart of the administration just as much as on that of the villagers. To begin and end rural development with purely technical work is not enough. Improved techniques and prosperity need a social revolution if the impetus is not to wither away. For example, women have to be educated, because female obscurantism can defeat the most zealous of reformers. The young must be given a social life if they are not to leave the village for the town as soon as they are educated; they must be provided with a forum where they can use their minds so that they do not forget what they have learned; they must also have an opportunity to earn a little money so that they may be less dependent on their elders. The American 4-H Clubs have been tried in India, without much success, because they were transplanted wholesale. The Indian replica of the 4-H Club must be Indian.

Community Projects take delicate handling, indeed. The Government is not always aware of this fact, as was shown in the remark of an official to Albert Mayer. He did not see why, if there were five successful projects in operation, there could not be five hundred a year from now. Mayer explained in vain that in order to go really fast, one must go slowly at first, that the present need is to put the brakes on a program that is rushing ahead without sufficient regard to the realities of resources and personnel. The real bottleneck is the shortage of men. If the Project staff is good and arouses the villagers' response, India's battle is half won; if, on the other hand, the staff is merely making a show to impress a politician or to get a quick promotion, the battle is unfought and the future is as dark as before. Today, every Member of Parliament, every member of the State legislatures, every Opposition candidate clamors to have a Community Project in his area. In October 1952, there were a handful of Community Projects. By 1961, the whole of India is to be covered either by the Community Projects or by the National Extension Service. (The Community Projects are a temporary concentration of personnel in one area; after four years the personnel is shifted to another area. The National Extension Service is a permanent organization which is far less concentrated in personnel. Its aim is to put within the reach of the village level worker a corps of specialists — such as a veterinarian, a sanitary inspector, a doctor, a crop expert — who can be called in at any time. These specialists do not stay in a small area; they are at the local headquarters and come only when called or to visit the village level worker on the spot.)

It was Gandhi who had insisted that India lives in her villages, but it was Albert Mayer who, more than any single individual, has provided the Government with the combination of techniques that has made it possible for them not to forget Gandhi's priorities. Had it not been for the technique for improving the village provided by the Community projects, the Government of independent India — racing with the West for skilled technicians, jet engines, and huge dams — might conceivably have forgotten how really important the village is. It might have tried unsuccessfully to solve India's ills by forcing the pace of industrialization, which would have been as hopeless a solution as attempting to scoop out the Indian Ocean with a ladle. The Community Projects have made rural development so successful and politically so compelling that the Indian budget has struck a balance between the expenditures on spectacular or strategic needs and those to raise the villagers' standard of living. The Second Five-Year Plan already provides four hundred million dollars for Community Projects.

Indeed, the danger is not that Albert Mayer's dream will be forgotten but that it will materialize too soon. The Indian villager is most responsive to new methods the first time he hears of them; but he will not listen a second time if the new method or idea fails, for he has no land with which to indulge in the luxury of experiment. My husband, for example, had an unfortunate experience when, on the advice of the Agricultural Department, he introduced a new strain of cotton into West Kandesh. He pushed the new crop hard and succeeded beyond his expectations. It was a roaring success everywhere, except on the strips of red soil just below the Satpura Range. Those villagers were so disgusted that he could get no further co-operation from them. He had not been told that this strain of cotton does not grow in red soil.

Today my husband's experience is not likely to be repeated. The Government of India and the State Governments are spending money on agricultural research and soil-testing; and the National Extension Service provides the scientist on an experimental farm with a field man whose duty it is to correlate research and practice. Before the villager is told to sow improved cotton on red soil, some of that soil is tried out back at the Government farm or, better still, on the spot.

16

The Dispossessed

One of the key factors of the Indian revolution is equality. To achieve it, the Government of India has not only to raise the status of the Harijans but to dispossess the rulers of the old regime of their power and privileges, while still making them a contented and integral part of the new India. Four groups of people have been especially subject to the process of dispossession: three pillars of the British regime — the princes, the landlords, and the public servants — and the businessmen.

Of these four groups, the most picturesque and the least powerful were the princes; the most dangerous politically were the landlords; and the most indispensable were the businessmen and the civil servants.

THE PRINCES

On 15 August 1947, when the British left India, there were 584 princes in India. In 1948, royal autocracy made way overnight for a lame, but nevertheless genuine people's democracy in that third of the subcontinent the British called 'Princely' India. The ninety-nine million people who lived in these regions were happy or unhappy, backward or advanced, according to whether they had a good or a bad king. Some kings ruled over territories as vast as England, Scotland, and Ulster; others, over an area the size of the Place de la Concorde or Washington Square. Some, like the Maharaja of Udaipur, had been kings since the glorious day when the Sun God had put his scepter in a warrior's hand; others, like some of the princelings of Kathiawar, were created by a British administrator who liked the dashing swagger of a land buccaneer.

Most beloved were the Maharajas of Cochin, who had a unique rule of succession to the throne: the eldest male member of the family was the heir. This meant that the average age of the rulers of Cochin was about seventy-five, and their reign was often as short as a Presidential term in the United States. Usually having not long to live, the aged rulers acted with restraint. These Maharajas earned their subjects' respect by their reluctance to wage war, their frugality with the State's treasury, and their just policies. Besides having mature rulers, the people of Cochin also enjoyed much pomp and ceremony, for state funerals and coronations were frequent. Whatever the exact reason, I have never seen such true affection between ruler and ruled as I saw in Cochin.

The next most popular ruler was the Maharaja of Mysore, whose great piety and statuesque deportment appealed to his devout subjects. His impromptu appearance in a crowd would create a respectful stir. Other rulers have been popular, bad though some actually were, because of their eccentricities. The sight of the old Maharaja of Patiala and his three hundred wives, walking in formation behind His Highness, dressed in those navy blue pajamas and sailor tops popular in the 1920's, tickled his people's sense of fun.

Whatever the popularity of individuals, if India was to be one nation and not five hundred and eighty-five nations, the princes could not continue as sovereigns after Independence. Yet, legally, they *were* sovereign. The first step was to persuade them to bring their territories within the Indian Union. Once in, they were prevailed upon to relinquish their sovereignty in exchange for a tax free pension. Today the Indian princes are subject to common law and to taxes, like every-

one else. Most important of all, they have just one vote apiece.
Their tax-free pensions and their taxable riches, which seem
to the Indians astronomical in an age of heavy taxation, are
in fact not very large. Many of them have regiments of pen-
sioners entirely dependent upon them for their daily food;
large numbers have tumble-down family palaces to maintain;
and, of course, most of them never had to keep track of their
money before. All in all, their funds are just sufficient to keep
them from bankruptcy or from turning Communist in despair. There are, of course, exceptions, such as the Maharajas
of Baroda, Gwalior, and Jaipur, all of whom own large quanti-
ties of industrial shares and have large bank accounts. These
few are rich in the modern as well as in the feudal sense. But
the old trappings of their wealth — diamond necklaces, polo
ponies, race horses, private airplanes, and elephants — are on
the way out.

In place of the old princes, a new and quite important little
group of politicians and technicians is emerging. Sons of
princes are now studying agriculture and engineering. Also,
many princes ran for office in 1951 and again in 1957 and
were elected.

One of the Maharajas had foreseen it all, years before but,
like Cassandra, he was not heeded. At the end of the war he
explained to me that feudalism was dead, that the only hope
for the princes was to anticipate the politicians:

'We must give adult suffrage to our people; we must pension ourselves off as if we were Ministers; and we must turn
our lands into Crown property and ourselves into trustees of
the people. We have tradition on our side. We do not need
political office. We will be more honest than politicians who
are in today, out tomorrow — many with no income outside
politics. We, too, are patriots. Patriotism was not invented by
Gandhi.'

Both of us knew that he was right and that he would fail
to convince his fellow rulers. When we met again in 1950, he
looked many years older, and the hand that held a glass was

thin, with blue veins bulging. We discussed the scale of compensation the Ministry of States was working out for princely power. 'The rulers are letting themselves be hanged with these financial strings,' he said. 'We ought to stand on our dignity like men and tell the Congress: "Take away your bribes. Let us fight you at the polling booth like Indians." '

Some princes have done just this: They ran for office, but kept their pensions. My friend's comment on this practice was characteristically clear-sighted: 'We ought to give the pensions back. The people will hold our tax-free money against us. This money is very little, but politically it is worth a lot to our enemies.'

The transition from princely power to citizenship seems to have succeeded: for every prince who regrets his lost autocracy, ten are grateful for present comforts and, even with the loss of their power, they are still rather more privileged than most people. Nonetheless, their pensions are shrinking, scaled down for their heirs, and the princes are being forced more and more to invest in national bonds. Soon an Indian prince will resemble an old French *émigré*: He will be a man who has no power but who still thinks that the world turns around pedigree. Indeed, the princes were no more than a parenthesis in the history of India, a history to which, except for a few great houses like Udaipur, they contributed little but color.

THE LANDLORDS

The landlord is a different problem, and he has been brought into line by a novel device — bureaucratic red tape.

The land system in India was peculiar in that three groups of people, besides the tenant and the landlord in the Western sense, received an income from the land. These groups were called Jagirdars, Inamdars, and Zemindars. Amongst them they owned half of India before Independence. The primary right of the Jagirdar or the Inamdar was to the revenue on the land, rather than to the rent. The primary right of the Zemindar was to a rent which was fixed by statute and collected from a tenant who was often almost impossible to evict. These people were easy to dispossess, for their main connection with the land was the right to receive payments from those who tilled it.

The basis of all Indian land reform under the Congress Government is the simple slogan: 'Land to the tiller.' The methods of obtaining this objective have varied from State to State, but the same process is at work everywhere. More than one hundred and twenty acts have already been passed, in accordance with which the State governments buy the landlords out, compensating a poor one in full and a wealthier one in part. Landlords were allowed to keep the land that they themselves had under cultivation, while those who had not cultivated any of their land, but had merely collected rent for it, were allowed to keep enough to become medium-sized farmers.

Once the Government had dealt with these special cases, it had to tackle the far more difficult problem of tenancy and equality. Tenancy was a simple matter to solve in comparison with rural equality. For one thing, it was a limited problem. Only 12 per cent of India's rural population listed itself as 'mainly tenants' in the 1951 census, and only one fifth of the land was under tenancy. Until the Government took the tenants under its wing — in some parts of India this happened in the 1930's, for some only in the 1950's — they could be evicted without cause, and their rents were often exorbitant — usually half of the crop and in parts of Madras sometimes as high as three quarters of the crop. The first step the State governments took was to give the tenant security of tenure. At present he can be evicted only for a very few reasons, and in many States he has the right to buy out the land he cultivates, at a price fixed by the Government or by an impartial agency rather than by the landlord. Rents have been reduced everywhere in varying degrees — in Bombay to one sixth of what they were, but by only 45 per cent in Andhra.

In theory the tenant is better off than he used to be, but in practice there are still abuses. Many tenants have suffered from the law that gives the landlord the right to take back land tilled by tenants, if he wants to cultivate that land himself and is not already holding more than the maximum the law allows. In Hyderabad, where the aristocracy is unusually oppressive, more than half the tenants have been evicted. In other States, however, there has been no such glaring abuse of the loopholes of the law. On the whole, evictions have been made principally for the bona fide resumption of land.

Equality follows tenancy reform. In India land has a value that goes far beyond mere economics. Seventy per cent of the population depends on agriculture for its livelihood, and this percentage is far more than India's agriculture can profitably support. During the last forty years the population on the land has nearly doubled. The land available has not increased by anywhere near that proportion. Although the figures are unreliable, probably the amount of land available has increased no more than one sixth. Even irrigation has gone up less than one third, and that rise largely in the last five years. The result is that half of India's farmers own less than five acres, and only 1 per cent owns more than fifty acres. The half with fewer than five acres owns about one sixth of the cultivated land, which is only as much as is owned by the 1 per cent of the farmers owning more than fifty acres. The remaining two thirds of the land is owned by people with from five to fifty acres. Finally, at the bottom of this scale is the one person in five who owns no land at all. Fifty acres is a very small farm in the United States and just barely a medium-sized farm in Europe, but in India it is very large. The Indian with fifty acres compares to his neighbor who has only half an acre as a Long Island millionaire compares to a Mississippi share-cropper. Nearly all the politicians and most educated Indians agree that equality cannot be founded on such a contrast in fortune.

The most difficult aspect of this situation is that the bigger landowner cannot be expropriated by fiat. Such a policy would go against the deep-rooted Indian belief that it is wrong to take away a man's livelihood and immoral to confiscate property. Even the largest landowner has the right to 'enjoy.' It would, moreover, be politically dangerous to deprive these landowners of their land, for they would then have the sympathy of their caste fellows, who would see the position of the entire caste threatened by the ruin of its leaders. In addition, if the large landowner was a widow, an orphan, a retired soldier, or pious, or merely respected, the whole village would be offended if the Government took away his or her property. The politician can never forget that the bigger peasants — the fifty-acre owners — are often the most respected people in the village. They are the backbone of society, and it is upon their influence that a political party must count. They will beat the drums for the candidates — and often they are the candidates.

Yet it is not feasible for them to remain so glaringly rich. It is politically unwise for them to make as much as two hundred dollars a month while many people around them earn only ten. But a drastic solution to the problem entails the grave risks of riot and of lower production. After all, the bigger farmer is often a better agriculturist, for he has the spare land on which to try out a new crop. The success or the failure of his experiments will determine whether the rest of the village sows improved onions or tries green manure. He can afford to buy fertilizer, for his credit is good. Indeed, he is usually the unofficial banker of the village, and his status is measured to some extent by the number of people to whom he lends, not always at high rates — he gets his prestige from their dependence rather than his profit.

By going slowly and tackling feudalism and tenancy on the land first, the Government has given the larger landowner time in which to split up his property into as many parts as he has trusted relatives. This has the advantage that the land will be in better hands with the owners' educated relatives, who usually have money enough to run it and understanding enough to adopt new techniques, than in the hands of a man who was not too long before a landless laborer. Meanwhile, the big farmer realizes that his days are numbered, that sooner or later a ceiling will be put on the amount of land he can own. This time will come soon.

Because over 250 million Indians are dependent on land and there are just over 300 million acres of land to be divided among them, there is general agreement in the Government that no one should be allowed to have a large share of this vital resource. There has been considerable agitation over the question of ceilings on land, but it is typical of the way things are done in India that the question has never been whether or not there should be a ceiling but how large the ceiling would be. The large landowner has devoted so much energy to insuring that he will keep as much land as possible that he has made no effort to argue against ceilings altogether. He is only concerned with seeing that the ceiling will not be less than thirty acres of reasonably good land, which is the figure that most of the States are likely to set. He will be so happy if it is not less that he will accept this without a murmur.

THE BUSINESSMEN

Two kinds of Indian businessman exist. First, there is the small businessman, who is either a small shopkeeper or a factory owner operating in his own backyard with no overheads. He usually has a loud voice at election time and must therefore be treated gingerly by the Government. He escapes most of the rigors of Government control and with his limited ability makes a lot of money compared with other members of the middle class. Second, there is the large operator — rich, vulnerable, and few in number. He has only one asset in his favor, and because of that, the Government cannot afford to ignore him, much as it would like to: he is irreplaceable at this stage in India's development. His government can tax him and control him, but it never dares make his life so miserable that he will stop producing or that the public will stop investing. The Government judges how far it can go by the Stock Exchange. If there is a crash, it goes easier straightway, for it wants all sections of the economy to develop. But the Stock Exchange would have to crash resoundingly for the Government to give the entrepreneur real freedom, as the entrepreneur is so much a pariah that even his shareholders seem to want the Government to control him.

The public is little disposed to tolerate businessmen. Hindu tradition despises those who care for the fruit of their labor, and is not a dividend a fruit? There are also reasons other than tradition. The Indian businessman has inspired little faith. During the war years, he was often a blackmarketeer, a tax evader, and a robber baron. The Indian businessman is viewed with jaundiced eyes in India, perhaps because he started late and so still tends to have the standards and methods of the nineteenth century.

Many of India's businessmen are like the American businessmen of the 1890's: enterprising but not always honest; they evade taxes and exploit labor. That is, however, only half the story. Along with its black sheep, the business community has many forward-looking, industrious men. The public, however, sees only the dishonesty, and it is too ready to damn the whole flock for the sins of its conspicuous rascals. Yet even the rascals have helped to start an industry where there was none before. Since they do it for profit, though, their enterprise is counted against them almost as much as their unscrupulousness.

It is owing to this attitude of the public that the Government does not confine itself to catching and punishing a dishonest businessman, but nationalizes the entire business sector concerned so that others will not be encouraged to cheat. If just one thief is caught and punished, the public thinks that many other thieves are carrying on scot-free. But the public applauds the Government's measures to restrict opportunities to steal.

This happens all the time, and no businessman is ever

credited with anything good. Some of India's businessmen
have taken real risks to improve Indian business and have
done so largely for patriotic reasons. There is the example of
Mr. Birla, who started many industries that people thought
were too advanced for India. The public did not admire his
foresight when he very sensibly used the reserves of a cotton
mill — the Government is limiting the expansion of cotton
mills — to start a rayon plant. Instead, it sneered and hoped
that the Government would protect their interests as shareholders from such as he. The Government does not have to
preach to the public against businessmen; instead, it has to
see that it is not pushed too far against them by the electorate.

Cutting the businessman or industrialist down to size is
part of the movement toward equality which is pervading
Indian life. His taxes are steadily rising. They first went up
annually with each Budget; now they are raised every time
money is needed for a new project such as producing steel
or expanding educational facilities. There are few people
besides the businessman who can be taxed directly and, if
indirect taxation is to increase — as it does all the time —
it is a political necessity to slice off the higher incomes. Under
a million people pay direct taxes in India, and with the extension of land reforms, the higher incomes are becoming
increasingly confined to urban and industrial areas. Nowhere
in the world do so few pay so much for so many. They will
have to pay much more before equality grows from a constitutional hope to a living fact.

Industry is also entangled with thousands of Government
controls and regulations. This is partly to avoid the misuse
of scarce resources — especially capital, the scarcest of all —
and partly to make the public feel that its interests are in safe
and clean hands. Thus, even the direction of industry is part
of the process if equalization which is reorganizing India's
traditional society into a brave new world. My little boy once
explained it to his American grandparents: 'Canned asparagus
is both expensive and rare in India because if it were only

expensive the rich could eat asparagus every day and the poor would feel so much poorer.'

Whenever I read of a new tax, a new regulation on industry, or a new step in the direction of austerity and State control, I remember that India is desperately poor and that it is all really a matter of asparagus.

THE PUBLIC SERVANT

The public servants — the civil servants, the policemen, and the Army — submitted to the new regime not because they feared worse would come but out of patriotism and ingrained loyalty to authority. Nevertheless the transfer of power meant for them a serious loss of position. Previously they had shared power with the British Parliament. A soldier was defense member; civil servants were governors of provinces and members of executive councils. Now politicians have taken over the power of the British Parliament and of the old public servants, who had to relinquish the reins of authority almost overnight. If they had sulked or served the new Indian Government grudgingly just to earn their pay, the new nation might have collapsed. And certainly it would have collapsed under the strain of its various crises — Partition, the Punjab massacres, the eight million refugees, the tribal invasion, the undeclared war with Pakistan in Kashmir, and bad monsoon seasons — if the Army had been discontented or the bureaucrats divided by intrigues.

It was not easy to assimilate the public servants and the politicians into one group. One of the main sources of popularity of the Congress leaders was that they had been in British jails. The State officials were often the men who had put them in jail. Moreover, the Congress Party and the old public servants had certain deep differences of outlook and background. A senior administrator once told Nehru that his colleagues were complaining because they were not promoted regularly, in respect to seniority. He explained that a civil servant does not like to intrigue or speculate in order to get on; he prefers the security of regular promotion. After listening attentively, Nehru smiled disarmingly and replied: 'You may be right, but you must realize that for a generation that has spent most of its adult years in jail security is a word that does not exist.'

There are other differences between politician and public servant. The officials, the civil servants especially, were on the whole better educated and came from a higher economic class than the average Congress man. These officials also valued the gracious living the British had introduced to India — from flower gardens to Western furniture, from cigarettes and an occasional drink to Western clothes. They shared, too, their British colleagues' belief that the Government knows best what is good for the people. By contrast, the Congress Party men make a fetish of austerity, renunciation, abstinence, and handspun cloth for their clothes; they believe that only men like themselves know what is good for the people.

Further, for thirty years, the Congress Party had been attacking not only the official's power but his pay. The old public servants who remained after Independence were given Constitutional guarantees for their pay. These guarantees left their salaries no higher than they were before the war, although the cost of living is three and a half times over the pre-war level. Officials appointed since Independence are paid much less. Only officials at the level of messengerboys, police constables, and the most junior of clerks are as well off — or perhaps even slightly better off — as they used to be. The senior official's standard of living has dropped by a half or more. Bungalows have been split up and the best ones given to Ministers. Only the most senior officials can travel in airconditioned accommodations.

It might seem that this was not the best way to command loyal service. Yet the public servants have been loyal, perhaps more than ever before. The Army endeared itself to the Congress Party by its steadfastness during the Partition troubles, its heroism in Kashmir, its readiness to help in every natural calamity, and its invariable good behavior. Indian civil servants have worked twelve and fourteen hours a day. India is still one of the best administered countries in the world. The civil service is overstrained, it has too much to do, it is still suffering from the break in recruitment during the war. There is still too much political interference and too much corruption on the lower levels, but, despite its defects, it is a more admirable machine than it ever was, for it now performs many new economic duties besides continuing its traditional job of keeping law and order.

17

Nehruism: Revolution by Consent

India today is undergoing a unique revolution. It is the world's only revolution to develop through democracy and by law. It is so successful that it is almost unnoticed. Yet, by the time it is over, India will be transformed from a thoroughly hierarchic society into one almost as firmly egalitarian as Sweden. Moreover, the Indian revolution — which is perhaps best described as 'Nehruist' because it owes so much to Mr. Nehru — will provide the rest of the under-developed world with a pattern of growth that will make Communism look old-fashioned and barbarian by comparison.

The Indian revolution lacks class warfare; it is a revolution by consent. The will of the small intelligentsia at the top takes effect only after the majority of the people have been convinced that they want to go along with their leaders. This revolution's weapon is not the terror of a police state but a series of legal acts which are interpreted by an impartial judiciary quite separate from the executive branch of the Government. It may move more slowly than a violent upheaval such as the Chinese Communist revolution, for it takes time to win popular consent. It also moves more surely, for, once consent is given, everyone, both conservative and radical, joins to support the new *status quo*. In contrast to China, India has neither counterrevolutionaries nor *émigrés*.

The Indian revolution is deliberately and avowedly Socialist,

but Socialist in a rather special way, with the emphasis on
equality rather than on state ownership of the means of production, distribution, and exchange. It attaches great importance to co-operation. It is conventionally Socialist mainly in
that it assumes that the State will take the initiative in economic development and planning, an assumption which will
end in making the state the driving force in Indian economic
life.

This role of the State distinguishes India's Socialism from
that of Scandinavia and England. The Socialist parties in the
West have also worked toward equality — indeed, there is
far more equality in Scandinavia than is either tolerable or possible in a country as poor as India — and the Welfare State is
their ideal. India's Welfare State is in its infancy, whereas the
Western Socialist nations already have fully developed welfare
economics. The real difference between India and Europe, however, is that Europe's Socialist parties developed in a capitalist
system, whereas India's Socialism has grown in a society where
capitalism still touches only the fringes. The labor parties
of England and the Scandinavian nations have learned by
experience that it is best to maintain private enterprise as the
mainspring of material progress. India, on the other hand,
never had a functioning capitalist economy, and it sees no
reason to develop one now. As a result, it is depending more
and more on the State as the planner, as the provider of
capital, and as the industrial entrepreneur.

There is no element of Russian Communism about the
Socialism of the Indian revolution. The Congress Party does
not believe in dialectical materialism or in class war; its supporters are not atheists; anti-clericalism is not an Indian issue;
Congress Party men have a positive abhorrence of violence.
The Congress aim is to save the capitalist from himself, to
use and transform him in the new regime — not to exterminate
him. Most important, the rule of law is as important in repub-
lican India as it was under the British. The Government might
often be able to move more quickly if it acted arbitrarily, but

it has specifically bound itself not to act so. The Constitution gives the individual citizen the right to equality before the law, to property, to religious and cultural freedom, and to the prerogative writs, such as habeas corpus. The Government has respected the Constitution scrupulously. Nehru does not hesitate to tell his people that totalitarian methods might sometimes be speedier, but that the extra slowness of the Indian way enables India to change and yet remain free and democratic in the process.

Democracy is another mark of India's Socialism that distinguishes it from the Communism. The Indian Government is elected by universal suffrage. Men and women, touchables and untouchables, Brahmins and aboriginals, all have one vote — and only one vote. This suffrage is not, as it has been in some nations, a sham. It is exercised regularly. Moreover, the electorate changes its mind and defeats ministers of whom it does not approve. At the 1951 general election it defeated no fewer than twenty-eight such ministers, including two Chief Ministers, while still returning the Congress Party to power. Parties, too, go up and down. The Communists won forty seats in Andhra in 1951; four years later, they won only thirteen in a house whose seats had increased by more than a third. In 1957 they won enough seats to form the Government in the State of Kerala. As Dr. John Matthai — ex-director of India's biggest business, ex-Finance Minister of the Government of India — put it: 'One has to be in Kerala to realize how widespread is the sense of relief, not that Communism has arrived but that Congress domination has, for the time being, come an an end.'

The checks that are imposed upon the Government can be very real at times. For example, the courts held that parents have the right to choose the language in which they want their children to be taught. Another time they decided that property must be taken over at its current market value and not at the prices of 1946. Some of these decisions, notably those involving compensation, have been met by alterations

of the Constitution or of the law, but the executive branch
of the Government has never defied the courts, nor has it tried
to impose its will regardless of the law.

Policy also is changed to satisfy the electorate. The Central
Government does not like the ban on cow slaughter, but
nonetheless many States have responded to public opinion and
banned cow slaughter. Again, the Central Government does
not like the loss in revenue that results from Prohibition, for
it drastically reduces the money available for development.
Prohibition is so popular with the public, however, that it
may well soon be extended over all of India. Then, the Central Government feared that State boundaries based on language, rather than on administrative convenience, would mean
States that were not altogether loyal to the Union; but, since
the public demanded that the Federation be reorganized so
that only one language be spoken in each State, the map of
India has been redrawn accordingly. Only the State of Bombay
is bilingual; and a large part of the electorate has made known
its displeasure at this one exception.

Naturally these aspects of Indian political life did not
spring full-grown from Nehru's head in 1947. They go deep
into the past — to the eighteenth-century British High Courts,
to Macaulay's Penal Code and Minutes on Education, and to
the Government of India Acts of 1919 and 1935, with their
provisions for larger electorates and increasingly responsible
government. Above all, they go back to Mahatma Gandhi.
Gandhi had boundless patience. He was endlessly willing
to negotiate, haggle, bargain, wait, ask and ask again, until
the enemy gave way in sheer weariness and the barriers fell.
This was true whether the enemy was the British or popular
prejudice against the Harijans or a lack of faith in nonviolence.
Gandhi taught Nehru the value of unformulated principles
and strategic retreats — provided the objective is never lost
to view. It was he, too, who developed, perhaps on a British
model, the technique of progressive change in which one
merges the best of the old with the new until even one's

victims are one's willing collaborators. Nehru has been an apt
pupil.

This Indian way of peaceful change and development without terror has the lasting advantage of being an indigenous
way and not a borrowed foreign one, as was the Chinese revolution. It is a way inspired by Gandhi and by the British law
and government practice, and by a centuries-old practice of
local self-government. Above all, the Indian way draws much
of its inspiration from Hinduism and from the Hindu attitude
to life. Indians do not like to enforce upon others decisions
made by a self-appointed body of men who claim to know
what is best for everyone. Hindu history is not one of feudalism, religious wars, and barricades, but of tolerance and per-
suasion. India's national day is not 15 August, the day the
British left India in 1947, but 26 January, the day the Republic
was proclaimed in 1948. Rather than celebrate the conquest
of the old regime, Indians celebrate the beginning of the
new.

Two pieces of personal history symbolize Indian tolerance.
Little more than ten years ago, Madame Vijaya Lakshmi
Pandit toured the United States to tell Americans of British
iniquities in India and thus gain sympathy for the Congress
Movement. At the same time, Sir Girja Shankar Bajpai, who
was the British Government's Indian Representative in Washington, was telling Americans how Congress Party policies
harmed the war effort. After Independence, both became
distinguished representatives of free India. Today Madame
Pandit is a popular High Commissioner of the Indian Government stationed in London, and, until his health gave way,
Sir Girja Shankar was India's senior Advisor on Foreign
Affairs.

In every area of reform, the Government is willing to change
conditions slowly by taking people along as fast as they are
able to go, rather than by driving them forward before they
are prepared to move. Thus, the Prime Minister was eager
to put the Hindu Code Bill into effect, but to put it through

at once in its entirety would have been going too fast for most orthodox Hindus. The divorce provisions aroused the opposition of President Rajendra Prasad, a devout and highly respected Hindu, who threatened to resign (and thereby split the Congress Party) unless the issues of the Bill were first presented to the electorate. Nehru could have forced the Hindu Code Bill through anyway, but he preferred to split it into sections. Each section was voted on separately by the people only after the ground had been well prepared in advance by propaganda. One after another, the sections have been approved.

Because of the Hindu Code Bill, the Hindu woman today is the equal of the Hindu man. She is the equal of her husband; she inherits from him. She need no longer depend on the charity of grudging in-laws. The Hindu woman has also become the equal of her brother. She can no longer be forced to get married or stay with her husband or his family.

The Hindu Code Bill is merely a further example of that cornerstone of Congress policy — equality. In the new India, everyone is of equal value and is to be given an equal opportunity. The principle of equality is based as strongly on the belief that inequality is immoral as on the political recognition that to perpetuate inequality is to invite violent revolution. The Government is raising the underprivileged through education and legislation. Many aspects of this policy have been discussed in the chapters entitled "The Dispossessed' — how new laws have gnawed away wealth and privilege, how the power of old officials has been curbed without loss of either the officials or their loyalty, how the most sweeping revolution of all, land reform, has curtailed the power of landlords and turned tenants into landowners. Even more revolutionary in implication are the Community Projects and National Extension Blocks which will cover the whole country by 1961. The Government takes the village in as an equal partner in these projects, and every change is made only when the villagers are prepared to accept it. These are all factors in the political revolution which is transforming the nation.

India's revolution is officially encompassed within its Five-Year Plans. Planning is an old Congress Party hobby which became universally popular at the end of the war — particularly in Delhi, Bombay, and other State capitals, where all the Government departments were making plans for the development of the economy. When the Congress Party took over from the British, it sifted out the more feasible of these plans and incorporated them into what became known as India's First Five-Year Plan. It was four years before the Government issued the Plan, however, because of the time it took to draw it up and to make the people sufficiently plan-conscious to accept the financial sacrifices involved. Even then, the Plan was more a priority list for Government expenditures than a real program.

The aims of the First Five-Year Plan were to prevent the Government from squandering money and to set out in general terms the ideals of social and economic equality that are so dear to the Congress Party. There was practically no planning for industrial expansion, beyond a list of the different activities the Government wished to encourage. If the Plan had failed, planning might well have been set aside for a long time, but it was a success and the people are now enthusiastic about it. The Second Five-Year Plan will be twice as extensive as the First, with a large Government investment in heavy industry as a new feature. There is a large gap between India's financial resources, internal as well as external, and its Second Plan, but India will not allow that to stand in her way on the road to equality with the more highly developed industrial nations.

What is happening in India has no exact parallel with anything in the West, for the revolution is fundamentally Indian, steeped in the great Hindu traditions of tolerance and non-violence — seeing some truth in all points of view and bringing final ruin to no one. Its keynotes are consent and equality.

18

The Irrelevance of Communism

India has none of the preconditions of Communism except poverty. It is a great misconception to group it with Russia and China as a backward peasant country ripe for violent revolution. There are aspects of the Hindu way of life which are basically inimical to the methods and aims of Communism.

Hindus are loath to take life; people who will not squash a cockroach, not out of squeamishness but because of a vague 'fellow-feeling,' are unlikely to run large scale 'liquidations.' This does not mean that Hindus are never violent. India has its riots. But, outside of professional bandits, such killings as occur in India are usually the result of hot blood, of a sudden blinding rage followed by a complete return to normal conditions. The Indian has a firm reluctance to use force as a means of settling difficulties.

Indians also are most willing to accept their fate. Often this willingness is carried to fantastic lengths. During the Bihar Famine of 1951 I saw bags of rice left unguarded, piled man-high along the river bank, waiting for the ferry to deliver them to the other side. Something must have gone wrong with the ferry, for two days later the bags were still there, still unguarded. It was almost unbelievable that the bags were still intact, for all around this mountain of food people were actually dying of hunger. Mothers who no longer had milk fed their infants jute leaves and slugs; grown-ups were chewing roots even cattle would not eat, and all the while these bags of rice stayed along the river bank for two whole days. I could not help feeling contempt for these wretched creatures. What did these mothers fear? Why did they not stir to save their children?

When I snorted at such complete apathy, a village elder replied, 'This rice is for others in the interior who need it more than we do. Once the river swells, they will be cut off for months. It would be wrong for us to steal from our brothers.' Then he asked a question which was followed by a hungry belch, 'Do you think our rice will come soon?'

This is not the only example. For instance, in the Bengal Famine of 1943, in which three million people died because they had nothing to eat, not one single grainshop, not one single godown, not one single silo was looted; in some places, thanks to the ineptitude of a corrupt administration, grain was rotting because its price was too high; yet not one single person — not one — felt hungry enough to rebel against fate. Whenever I have chafed at this acceptance of fate, at this disproportionate respect for law and order, my Indian friends, Western-educated though they are, have looked at me with exactly the same stare as my Bihar villager when he said, 'It would be wrong for us to steal from our brothers.' The Marxian class war can have little appeal for a people who quietly lie down in the dust and cease to live rather than help themselves to an unguarded bag of rice.

India is steeped in its religion. Moreover, Hinduism is a creed of tolerance. It provides the illiterate villager with a way of life which satisfies his needs. It provides the educated with a philosophy which he can reconcile with his belief in the need for the modern outlook. The tug-of-war which, for example, Israel is fighting between its orthodox and its progressive citizens does not arise, perhaps because there is no organized priesthood in Hinduism. In addition, both the Hindu scriptures and the Hindu ascetic stress the value of renunciation and preach the perfecting of the individual soul by humility and detachment.

Hinduism, unlike the Biblical religions, does not concern itself with the lot of the masses (to this extent the Judeo-Christian tradition is a more favourable background for Communism than Hinduism). This detachment from society comes from the belief that man is paying in his present life for actions in lives past, that to interfere with the payment is to interfere with the ways of God. A Harijan's duty is to be a good Harijan, not to behave as a Brahmin. It may be that as caste collapses, if it ever does, India will become more susceptible to Communism. But it will take a very long time before India has a casteless society. Meanwhile, the very factor which spikes the wheels of progress in India — Hindu orthodoxy — is also a major bulwark for stability.

The intellectuals, whom Marx called the 'vanguard of the intelligentsia,' are not as fatalistic and law abiding as the villagers, for they have been contaminated with traces of Western materialism. But they have no reason to revolt; their revolution is over. They are the Government, the politicians, the bureaucrats, the technicians. Their views carry a quite disproportionate influence in framing India's future.

Labor, which Marx lumped together, by calling it 'proletariat,' is both heterogeneous and pampered in India. It is often necessary to use five different languages in one factory, because the workers come from different parts of the country. Even if they belong to the same state, they come from different castes, so that it is never easy to make them feel as a 'proletariat' should. But even were it possible, they are far too well off — relatively — and far too protected to storm any Bastille. An unskilled floor sweeper or pusher of a cart in a Bombay factory gets twice as much as a primary school teacher; a factory worker cannot be sacked (even if caught stealing) without the most cumbersome formalities, and retrenchment is practically impossible, except for the Government, or sometimes, by the payment of large gratuities. Large firms are helping to raise the standard of living by paying well above the market level. The skilled working class is imperceptibly beginning to emerge as India's new middle class — the class with leisure, the class that goes to the movies and owns bicycles.

The Welfare State is coming into being in India. The wide gulf between rich and poor, which bred Communism in Russia and China, is being vigorously attacked by the Indian Government. Very few people in India today are really rich, and those few are fast disappearing. Effective measures for leveling down income are being taken. The income-tax is higher than it is in the United States; death duties, a capital gains tax and a wealth tax have been introduced; a beginning has been made toward a comprehensive state insurance law. The Government is working rapidly to eliminate the bases on which Communism has been built in other countries. Through constitutional measures to insure equality, through taxation, through ceilings on landholding and perhaps one day on income the Government is taking more active steps than the Communists to usher in a classless society.

Both in China and Russia, the peasant's thirst for land was overpowering, and the Communists began by giving him the land as an expedient to get the power which would enable them to take it back later. In India, there is not the same sort of thirst for land (although there is not enough to go around). Perhaps two thirds of India's peasants own all or most of the land they cultivate, and their proportion has been enormously increased by the anti-landlord legislation passed all over India. India is a country of very small peasant proprietors. The Communist slogan of 'Land to the tiller' is already Government policy.

Only the Harijans are possible material for a class war — indeed, in Andhra in the 1954 elections they mostly voted Communist — but even they are getting land of their own and will increasingly be treated as citizens. Even if they are not becoming equal, they are a minority everywhere and could not capture power so long as the Government governs and the Army is loyal. Moreover, against any Communist upsurge there would be the whole weight of India's society, which is not only deeply religious but is composed mostly of peasants owning three acres of land or businessmen owning a ten-cubic-foot shop.

Many experienced observers in India fear that India might go Communist through elections if the Communist ideology is accepted in the towns. They argue that if the urban intellectual and the urban proletariat go Communist, India will go Communist. This is not so. So long as there are free and fair universal-suffrage adult elections in India, it is not what the town but what the countryside thinks that matters. Calcutta is heavily Communist; Bengal, however, has a non-Communist Government.

Why should there be a Communist revolution when it is the Government in power which stands for progress and modernism? In India the Congress Government is the main protagonist of Westernization. It has an industrial program. It stands for hydro-electric schemes, heavy industry, and scientific agriculture. The Indian Army has not only some of the best soldiers in the world, it has an integral and respected part to play in the national life, and even the Communists dare not criticize this. Getting hold of the towns, therefore, is not getting hold of India; India has a Government that governs, an Army that carries out orders, and an electorate that votes.

This does not mean that there are no Communists in India or that India cannot go Communist. In the 1952 elections the Communists got 5 per cent of the total votes. In the 1957 elections they got nearly 10 per cent, and became the Government in one state — Kerala. But in Kerala the people voted not for the Communists but to protest against Congress corruption and the personality of the ex-Chief Minister, a man so hated that when the news of his defeat came through, people distributed sweets in the streets of the city. The Congress had made one long series of mistakes in Kerala, its leaders quarreled with each other, and it considered caste and religion to such an extent that appointments of Government officers had become impossibly involved and nepotic. Further, it had alienated the citizens of Trivandrum by refusing to allow them a High Court Bench after the formation of the new State of Kerala. More important still, it had failed to bring relief to the unemployed in the coastal districts and had sat on land reforms which had been formulated by the Socialists during their brief period of office.

The Communists did not promise the people of Kerala liquidations and Communism; they simply said: 'Vote for us and we shall give you a clean administration and an honest government. We shall try to create full employment and, if the Center lets us, we shall nationalize foreign-owned plantations.' Except for the nationalization of the plantations, their manifesto read like a mildly leftist version of the Congress's own. And, strangely enough, one of the first actions of this atheistic Marxist regime was to invite Acharya Vinoba Bhave to stay in Kerala and preach his reforms through love. Mr. Namboodiripad, the Chief Minister, attended the Saint's prayer meetings with great humility. Maybe he was merely playing up to his voters, but even if he was, his action still demonstrated how little genuine appeal Communism could have for the average Indian. It was the Communists who had to give in to Indian desire, and not vice-versa.

The Communists will not be a threat to the Government at the Center so long as Congress continues to govern reasonably well. The Communist Party of India has an inglorious past history. Before the last war it was part of the Congress Party. In 1939 it boycotted India's participation in the war, but, from the moment Russia was attacked by Germany, it supported the British in their war effort, making it clear that its allegiance was to Russia and not to India. Since 1947, it has had a purge every time Moscow has called a different tune.

The Communists, moreover, suffer from a severe handicap.

They are modern, agnostic, ruthless. The Indian villager is old-fashioned, religious, sentimental. The Communists often seem to forget this fundamental difference. They act as if India were in Europe and talk to the Indians as they would to Westerners. The result is a loss of influence, and, in an election campaign, a loss of votes. For example, a prominent Communist leader canvassed South India under the slogan: 'Vote for the party of the red flag and we shall harness the landlords' women to the plow.' In one village, he said this and then pointing to the wife of a landlord, who stood listening, with a golden chain around her neck he said, 'Instead of the mark of gold, her neck will bear the marks of hard work.' By that remark he lost his party tens of thousands of votes. The gold necklace is a sign of marriage. The villagers were horrified to hear that the Communists would harness women to the plow and deprive them of their wedding necklaces. If voting for the red flag meant that, they wanted nothing to do with Communism.

Just the same, one can never be finally sure. India can still go Communist if there is a world war, if the Second Five-Year Plan fails and the pressure of population becomes intolerable, or if the caste system with its religious accompaniments were to collapse suddenly, leaving nothing in its place. Fortunately none of these are likely to happen. India's great changes will in all probability take place within a political system closely allied to Western ideals. No one today can foresee what India will be a century from now. Only one thing is certain, it will be very different. Warm and reassuring as the old Indian world may be, it cannot remain. In today's world one must change or have change forced upon one. As the Japanese proverb says, 'One can never bathe in the same river twice.' If democracy fails, India will try something else.